A Closer Walk with JESUS

30 DAYS OF HOPE & INSPIRATION

a devotional journal

A Closer Walk with
JESUS

30 DAYS OF HOPE & INSPIRATION

a devotional journal

Travis & Tiffany Tombre

A Closer Walk with Jesus, 30 Days of Hope & Inspiration
Copyright © 2020 by Travis & Tiffany Tombre
First Edition: October 2020
Revision: November 2020

All rights reserved. No part of this book may be reproduced or transmitted in any form or by any means without written permission of the publisher, except in brief quotes or reviews. Unless otherwise noted, all Scripture is taken from the New International Version of the Bible® (NIV). Copyright © 1982 by Thomas Nelson. Used by permission. All rights reserved.

To order products, or for any other correspondence:

Hunter Entertainment Network
4164 Austin Bluffs Parkway, Suite 214
Colorado Springs, Colorado 80918
www.hunter-ent-net.com
Tel. (253) 906-2160 – Fax: (719) 528-6359
E-mail: contact@hunter-entertainment.com
Or reach us on Facebook at: Hunter Entertainment Network
"Offering God's Heart to a Dying World"

This book and all other Hunter Entertainment Network™ Hunter Heart Publishing™, and Hunter Heart Kids™ books are available at Christian bookstores and distributors worldwide.

Chief Editor: Gord Dormer
Book cover design: Phil Coles Independent Design
Layout & logos: Exousia Marketing Group www.exousiamg.com

ISBN: 9798550558263
Printed in the United States of America.

Dedication

We dedicate this book to those who want a closer walk with Jesus. May the testimonies and biblical truths within these pages bring you a fresh wind of hope and encouragement, and strengthen you on your journey with the Lord.

Acknowledgments

We would like first to give glory to God. We are humbled and honored to be used by Him to advance the Kingdom through this book's writing.

We want to express our deepest gratitude to Mick Dubea for providing a platform for Travis to write weekly for his company. Because of Mick's compassion to see the men of his company know Jesus, Travis received the opportunity to minister through writing, which he would have never done otherwise.

Lastly, special thanks to the support and encouragement of our family and close friends. Thank you for believing in us to do what God has called us to do, for all the prayers and words of encouragement, and celebrating the milestones through this wild ride.

Foreword

There are books and resources I have consumed over my life with the Lord that has been pivotal and life-changing, and this book is one that I believe can be that for YOU, the reader. Tiffany and Travis are two people who press for the miraculous of God in their lives in a way that few do. The wisdoms and testimonies found in this devotional speak to their faith in God's faithfulness and is a reflection of their desire to share the fruit of their lives with others, so that the *price they paid* will continue to bear fruit for the Kingdom of God! Eat deeply of the wisdoms found in these pages, because it is not just "seeds" of truth you'll be tasting, but the fruit of lives who have walked the narrow road, the kind of stuff that will offer REAL nourishment to your spirit. This devotional (and the ones to come) will challenge your level of faith to new, life-changing places, and will help you also step into deeper places of knowing God personally, so that your life will also be a testimony of God's faithfulness to the world around you. Keep watching for more material from this couple... you will be glad you did!

Jenilee Samuel
Host of Java with Jen Podcast
Co-founder of Free Life Missions
Executive Pastor at Community Church in Orange, TX.

Table of Contents

Introduction 1

<u>30 Days of Hope & Inspiration</u>

1. Do It Again 3
2. Let It Be 9
3. Sifted Like Wheat 15
4. God Remembered 21
5. Jesus Was Rejected 27
6. Heavenly Exchange 33
7. Never the Same 39
8. A New Thing 45
9. Follow the Instruction 51
10. Just Keep Walking 59
11. Give and it Will Be Given to You 65
12. Created to Praise 71
13. Word vs World 77
14. More Than You Can Handle 85
15. God Helps 91

16. The Lion and the Bear Trained David 97
17. Valley of Dry Bones 103
18. Finding God 109
19. Birthing Process 115
20. A Prosperous Soul 123
21. Travis's Testimony 131
22. God of the Impossible 137
23. Out of Egypt 143
24. Man, of a Different Spirit 147
25. Jim's Testimony 153
26. Possessing Your Promised Land 161
27. Slaying the Giants 167
28. 12 Spies 173
29. Mary Moments 179
30. The Good Shepherd 185
Bibliography 191
About the Authors 193

Introduction

Have you wondered what it was like to see Jesus walk on water? What did He write in the sand that day when addressing the crowd on the woman's act of adultery? Could you imagine being Zacchaeus in the tree, and Jesus calls you down and says, "I am coming to eat with you today?" Maybe you have thought; I would have loved to watch Jesus open the eyes of the blind, cause the dumb to speak, and the lame to walk. Oh, or how about witnessing Jesus calling a dead man to come alive again? What must it have been like to be the lady crippled by a spirit for eighteen years all of a sudden set free? Could you imagine being one of the twelve that walked with Jesus daily? Perhaps the questions on the table all lead to one answer—it is all obtainable through *a closer walk with Jesus*.

Throughout the Word of God, we read accounts of people having encounters with Jesus that transformed their walk with Him profoundly. The truth is Jesus longs to meet with us and tell us great and hidden things that we have not known. (Jeremiah 33:3) We are guessing that since you are reading this book, you want to have more intimate experiences with Jesus. Well, beloved, get ready to grow closer to Jesus and have encounters in the process, like those of the Bible!

We hope that you will experience *a closer walk with Jesus* on this 30-day journey as we dive deep into the Word of God to discover freedom, joy, deliverance, healing, wisdom, and understanding. Each daily devotional allows you to journal as you reflect, meditate, and evaluate your walk and guides you along a path toward a more intimate relationship with Jesus. Our goal is to equip you to transform your walk by understanding the power of applying God's Word to your lives and experiencing Jesus on a deeper level.

May the stories within these pages bring you a fresh wind of hope and inspire you to "A Closer Walk with Jesus."

30 Days of Hope & Inspiration

DO IT AGAIN

"Thus says the Lord, who makes a way in the sea And a path through the mighty waters." (Isaiah 43:16)

> I've seen You move, move the mountains
> And I believe I'll see You do it again
> You made away, where there was no way
> And I believe I'll see You do it again
> Your promise still stands
> Great is Your faithfulness, faithfulness
> I'm still in Your hands
> This is my confidence, You never failed me yet. (Do it Again by Elevation Worship[i])

As I was singing the lyrics to this song in worship Sunday, I began to reflect on the faithfulness of God. Oh, the mountains I have seen God move in my own life moves me to tears. When I was at my lowest, entangled in sin, God made way for me where there was no way. There have been situations my family has faced that, at the time, seemed dark and hopeless, yet God, in His faithfulness, made a way where there was no way. I am curious, like me, have you ever faced a problem in life where there seemed to be no solution? You felt like you have tried everything, and nothing seemed to give you the outcome you desired or desperately needed? You have labored and toiled all night and still came up short. Maybe it is in the area of finances or relationships? For some, the problem could be in school, with your children, or decisions to make within your career. Whatever problem we are facing, there is One who has and is the solution.

As we take a closer look at our key verse, we see that the Lord is in the business of making a way where there is no way. God makes a way in the wilderness and rivers in the desert. Where there is no clear path forward, our God creates one. Where the is no natural relief or refreshment, our God provides one! Our problems do not exhaust God's power! Let us take a walk through Scripture and watch how God specializes in showing His power in hopeless situations.

As the Egyptians pursue all Pharaoh's horses, chariots, and his army, the Israelites feared greatly and cried out to the Lord. God made a way, where there was no way. God displays His faithfulness by delivering the Israelites. Then, Moses stretched out his hand over the sea, and the Lord caused the sea to go back by a strong east wind all that night, and made the sea into dry land, and the waters were divided. And the Israelites went through the sea on dry ground, with a wall of water on their right and on their left. (Exodus 14:21-22)

After setting out from Elim, the Israelites complain against Moses for lack of food. God made a way, where there was no way. We see God graciously and faithfully provide. Then the Lord said to Moses, "Behold, I am about to rain bread from heaven for you, and the people shall go out and gather a day's portion every day." (Exodus 16:4)

Despite the King's unchangeable decree, he was forced to sentence Daniel to the den of lions. Daniel was left alone to face his destiny. God made a way, where there was no way. God's faithfulness to Daniel was affirmed. Then, Daniel said to the king, "O king, live forever! My God sent His angel and shut the lions' mouths so that they have not hurt me because I was found innocent before Him; and also, O king, I have done no wrong before you." (Daniel 6:21)

After Paul and Silas cast out demons in the name of Jesus and proclaim the way of salvation, orders from the magistrates were given for them to be beaten with rods. They inflicted many blows, and then they were thrown in prison. God made a way, where there was no way. Not only did the Presence of God filled those jail cells, bringing them comfort and joy amidst their suffering, but God's faithfulness to Paul and Silas was also justice rendered on their behalf. About midnight, Paul and Silas were praying and singing hymns to God, and the other prisoners were listening to them. Suddenly, there was such a violent earthquake that the foundations of the prison were shaken. At once, all the prison doors flew open, and everyone's chains came loose. But when it was day, the magistrates sent the police, saying, "Let those men go." And the jailer reported these words to Paul, saying, "The magistrates have sent to let you go. Therefore come out now and go in peace." (Acts 16:25-26, 34-36)

That day in the garden, when Eve saw that the fruit of the tree was good for food and pleasing to the eye, and also desirable for gaining wisdom, she took some and ate it. (Genesis 3:6) Though God's love for us is constant and unconditional, our sin separates us from spending eternity with Him. We all have sinned and fallen short of the glory of God. (Romans 3:23) We watch, through Scripture, God set in motion His plan to reclaim the lost. Long before He laid down Earth's foundations, He had us in mind, had settled on us as the focus of His love, to be made whole and holy by His love.

Travis & Tiffany Tombre

Long, long ago, He decided to adopt us into His family through Jesus Christ. (What pleasure He took in planning this!) He wanted us to enter into the celebration of His lavish gift-giving by the hand of His beloved Son. (Ephesians 1:4-6) God loves us so much that He gave His one and only Son, that whoever believes in Him shall not perish but have eternal life. (John 3:16) God made a way, where there was no way, being justified freely by His grace through the redemption that is in Christ Jesus. (Romans 3:24) Jesus is the way for us to receive God's grace and forgiveness. This is the ultimate act of God's faithfulness towards us. The most significant provision of making a way where there was no way, He sent us JESUS!

May we have faith to believe that the Lord makes a way where there is no way.

So, whatever mountain stands before you, whether it be a financial mountain, health mountain, parenting mountain, marriage mountain, or a mountain of addiction, cry out to God, and He will make a way where there is no way.

If you need refreshment, He will provide. If you need a clear path, He will create it. God is ever faithful. He is never changing.

"But this I call to mind, and therefore I have hope. The steadfast love of the Lord never ceases; his mercies never come to an end; they are new every morning; great is your faithfulness." (Lamentations 3:21-23)

He will do it again!

A Closer Walk With Jesus

JOURNAL/REFLECTIONS

1. What problems are you facing today?

_____
_____
_____
_____
_____
_____
_____
_____
_____

2. Which one of the people we talked about today gives you hope and why?

_____
_____
_____
_____
_____
_____
_____
_____
_____
_____
_____
_____
_____
_____

3. How is God making a way where there seems to be no way on your behalf?

_____
_____
_____
_____
_____
_____
_____
_____
_____
_____

Personal Prayer

_____
_____
_____
_____
_____
_____
_____
_____
_____
_____
_____
_____
_____

LET IT BE

"And Mary said, "Behold, I am the servant of the Lord; let it be to me according to your word." And the Angel departed from her." (Luke 1:38)

Out of curiosity, have you ever received a word from the Lord that left you scratching your head? I am speaking of a word from the Lord that you were like, "Hmm Lord, was that You? God, did I hear that correctly? You want me to do what? Surely, You got me mixed up with someone else, right?" Well, I will let you in on a little secret. I have experienced this more than once!

In some cases, it might be easy for us to question whether or not we heard from the Lord. If I find myself in this position, and I know I am seeking God for clarity or confirmation to the word spoken, I find comfort in the truth of the Word that says,

"My sheep hear my voice and do not follow the voice of another." (John 10:27)

This truth reminds me I am a sheep, and my Father is the Shepherd; therefore, I hear Him when He speaks. If we have struggled with this, we can take heart; we are not the only ones! We can stroll through Scripture and see that others, like Gideon, Moses, and Esther, initially questioned what God instructed them to do. (Judges 6, Exodus 3, Esther 4)

On the contrary, today, we will visit a woman who, when given details regarding her destiny, accepted without hesitation. A well-known first-century BC Galilean Jewish woman. A woman admired for her bravery and devotion to God. We can learn a lot from the experience of this woman, for she knew whose she was, and she trusted God deeply. Today, we will take a closer look at Mary, the mother of Jesus.

Let us imagine for a minute being in Mary's shoes. A teenage virgin girl betrothed to a man (the standard custom of the time was for girls to get married at a young age) has an angelic visitation where she's told that God chose her to give birth to the Savior of the World. Mary would overcome ridicule and opposition from those around her, as word spread of her being pregnant by the Holy Spirit with the Christ-child and not yet married. This young girl would give birth to this child who would go through life perfect, without sin! This child would one day walk on water, give sight to the blind, calm storms with His Word, walk where angels trod, cause the deaf to hear, the lame to speak, and the dead to live again. Mary would go on to raise this child, who was the Lord of all Creation, and who would one day rule the Nations. Mary would give birth to Heaven's perfect Lamb! Wow! The level of trust Mary had in God at such a young age is quite astounding! Mary exhibited incredible courage, humility, and a willingness to be used by God. She accepted an overwhelmingly huge responsibility to steward the call placed on her life by God with such confidence.

So, let us recap, an Angel of the Lord has just revealed to Mary that she will become pregnant by the Holy Spirit and carry the Son of God. (Luke 1:36-37) Our key verse should serve as an encouragement to us as we see how Mary responds to the instruction of the Lord. In verse thirty-eight, we see Mary's answer to the Angel of the Lord is a beautiful example of faithful discipleship in submission to God's Word. Mary, at that moment, was faced with making a life-changing choice. She could choose to forgo the call God was placing on her life and do her own thing, or surrender and fulfill her destiny. Right away, we see Mary's confidence in whose she is by her acknowledging her identity first. Mary boldly declares that she is a servant of the Lord. Because Mary understands that she belongs to the Lord, she knows she can trust God to help her fulfill her calling. For Mary to have had this degree of understanding as a young girl in that period was nothing short of a miracle.

When God asks us to do something for Him, we can trust Him to give us the grace to full fill it. (2 Timothy 1:9) It is so important, as children of God, that we know our identity is in Him alone. We are God's exclusive possession, and we have been crucified with Christ, and we no longer live, but Christ lives in us. (1 Peter 2:9, Galatians 2:20) What is worthy of noting next, is that Mary did not argue with what the Angel of the Lord said would take place. She did not try to convince God that He must have made a mistake. Mary comes into agreement with the call God placed on her life. Even if she did not understand the fullness of what the call placed on her life would look like, she chose to trust God anyway. As followers of Jesus, we have been set apart for the Kingdom of God.

We have been chosen and appointed to go and bear fruit that would last. (John 15:16) Jesus has saved us and called us to a holy life not because of anything we have done, but because of His purpose and grace. (2 Timothy 1:9) Mary's life was one that held great honor, but would also require great suffering. (Luke 2:35) She would experience the greatest joy in motherhood, but she would also experience a mother's most substantial pain. Mary would watch her Son perform miracles, signs, and wonders, blessing everyone who comes to Him. But we would also watch Mary rely on God's strength as she witnesses her sinless Son on the devastating journey to the Cross. She would watch Him hang on the Cross crucified, bearing the weight of the world's sin, fulfilling the prophecies spoken over Him from long ago. Yet, through it all, she never stopped trusting God.

Mary lived a life that shows us the grace of God will meet us no matter where we find ourselves. We all have a destiny to fulfill for the Kingdom and glory of God. Whatever God has called us to, He will bring us through. When we understand that we are children of God, we can walk in confidence and assurance that all He has for us is for our good and to bring Him glory. Whether we experience significant pain or sweetest joy, we can trust Him to be with us through it all. The power of submission to the will of God in our lives can have a significant impact on generations.

Next time the Lord gives us instructions, may we respond as Mary did. "Behold, I am the servant of the Lord; let it be to me according to Your Word."

A Closer Walk With Jesus

JOURNAL/REFLECTIONS

1. Has the Lord asked you to do something that seemed bigger than you?

___

2. John 10:27 says, "My sheep hear my voice and do not follow the voice of another." How does God speak to you?

___

3. How does Mary's response to God's instruction in Luke 1:38 encourage you to respond to what God is asking you to do?

___

Personal Prayer

___

SIFTED LIKE WHEAT

"And the Lord said, "Simon, Simon! Behold, Satan has demanded to have you, that he might sift you like wheat. But I have prayed for you, that your faith should not fail; and when you have returned to Me, strengthen your brethren." (Luke 22:31)

It was just another day for me. My husband was off to work, and I had set out to run around town, accomplishing my list of "to-dos". As I was walking down the grocery aisle, my phone rang. "Mrs. James, this is Don (he sounded panicked, but was trying to keep it together for my sake), and I wanted you to know that Ugh... Umm... Mark, well, he is okay. You do not need to worry, but we were working with him on a forklift, and Mark has fallen thirty feet off of it, and we are taking him to the emergency room to have his ankle looked at. Again, Mrs. James, don't worry; he is okay, and we will keep you updated."

The first step in the process of sifting wheat is to loosen the chaff from the grain. In Jesus' time, they would have harvested the wheat and placed it in some sack, laying it on the threshing floor and beating it violently with a flail. Once that step of the process was done, they then needed to separate the grain from the chaff. This would involve throwing the mixture into the air, so that the slightest wind would blow away the lighter chaff, causing the heavier grains to fall back down onto the floor.

Can you picture the process of sifting wheat in relation to how it might feel when we go through times of testing? May it feel like we are taking a beating ourselves, right? It might be hard to imagine that, as a follower of Jesus, we will also be sifted as wheat. It would be easier for us to focus on the truths that make us feel all warm and fuzzy like the goodness of God's love and grace, as opposed to those that might make us feel pretty uncomfortable. But today's key verse reveals a truth about the testing we should not ignore.

In Scripture, Satan has to be given permission by God to shake us violently, just as one does wheat. And God, in His Sovereignty, sometimes agrees. (Job 1:12) One of the ways we see Satan work is he tries the faith of believers to place temptations and trials in their way, that they may be tested. Thus, God gave Simon into his hands, that through this testing, his faith would not fail, and he would return to Christ. (Luke 22:32) God's purpose for these times of testing is always good. It is a process, just like the wheat, for anything to be removed from us that is not good or beneficial for us. When this testing takes place, there can be lessons to learn and growth to take place for our good. (Revelation 2:10) It is an opportunity where God's glory can be displayed in us and through us. In our weakness, God's grace is always sufficient for us. It is an invitation for us to continue to mature in our walk with the Lord. These testing's will prove our faith genuine. (1 Peter 1:7) God's desire for us is to be transformed into His image with ever-increasing glory. (2 Corinthians 3:18)

So, the question then is, "Where is God while we are being sifted?"

When we are in situations where we feel like we are being shaken, it can feel, or appear, like God is absent. On the contrary, He is not; He is right there with us in the middle of it. (Joshua 1:5) He has never left us nor forsaken us. Just like a teacher giving their students a test, the teacher sits and waits quietly. God is always for us and with us, even in the midst of testing time. God draws near to us through the intercessory presence of His Son, Jesus Christ. (1 Timothy 2:5, Luke 22:32)

Turns out that he did have a fractured ankle, but a few days later, it all got worse. My husband developed a 6-inch blood clot behind the knee. Part of this blood clot broke off and went to his lungs, causing him to have a pulmonary embolism, sending us straight to the emergency room. My husband was laid up for months not able to work, and I had to give him injections into his stomach to keep any of the blood clots from breaking off and going to his lungs or worse, his brain. We incurred thousands of dollars in medical debt, and over the next few months, we would be stretched in such a way that we were not expecting or truthfully, inviting.

You see, through this time of testing, we learned and grew so much! We quickly began to be reminded that our security was not in money, a job, a group of people, our even good health; it was in Jesus alone. We came to understand the truth a little deeper that the devil comes to kill, steal, and destroy, BUT Jesus came to give us LIFE MORE ABUNDANTLY. (John 10:10) We saw God use this time of testing to strengthen our marriage. There were many opportunities we found to praise God in the middle of this storm. We came to know God as Jehovah-Jireh, the "Lord who provides." The testimonies are numerous God gave us from the supernatural provision to God preserving and recovering my husband's body. We can testify He is El Roi, the "God who sees." Every time we called on the name of the Lord in time of trouble, we watched Him show up over and over and over in ways we could not have imagined. (Ephesians 3:20, Psalm 50:15) Yet, what we suffered then was nothing compared to the glory He revealed to us later. (Romans 8:18)

May I suggest that, sometimes, we ask God to deliver us from something, but God wants to carry us through something.

I love what Jude from *Truth Immutable* says, "The closing phrase of the verse reminds us that, as followers of Christ, we have the responsibility to serve Him. Nothing that happens in our lives – good or bad – is ever only for ourselves. When we are sifted as wheat, it is firstly to work in us to remove what is not of God. But its greater purpose is that we are prepared and able to strengthen others. Our experience will help others in their journey, and God empowers us through our trials to equip us to strengthen others. It is not optional. Jesus said that when we return, we must strengthen others. This responsibility is what empowers our struggle with supernatural kingdom power. Our victory in Christ is, therefore, multiplied. It adds compelling value to what we have gone through. But if we hold back and avoid the responsibility to 'pass it forward,' we work against the purposes of God."

So, if you find yourself in a season of being sifted like wheat, remember there is purpose, lessons, and growth in all of it for your good and God's glory. (Romans 8:28) The Lord is faithful, and He will strengthen and protect you from the evil one. (2 Thessalonians 3:3) God will protect you from trouble and surround you with songs of deliverance. (Psalm 32:8) He will Himself restore you and make you strong, firm, and steadfast. (1 Peter 5:10) As you come out of this testing time, may your faith be strengthened, so that you can go and strengthen others.

"For we do not have a high priest who is unable to sympathize with our weaknesses, but we have one who in every respect has been tested as we are, yet without sin. Let us, therefore, approach the throne of grace with boldness, so that we may receive mercy and find grace to help in time of need." (Hebrews 4:16)

A Closer Walk With Jesus

JOURNAL/REFLECTIONS

1. When was the last time you were sifted, and your faith was strengthened?

_____
_____
_____
_____
_____
_____
_____
_____
_____

2. Through your time of testing, how have you grown or what have you learned?

_____
_____
_____
_____
_____
_____
_____
_____
_____
_____
_____
_____

3. What might be the purpose God is trying to accomplish through this time of sifting?

Personal Prayer

GOD REMEMBERED

"Who remembered us in our low estate, For His lovingkindness is everlasting." (Psalm 136:23)

Have you ever found yourself in a season where you feel like the Lord does not hear your prayers? Maybe, you feel like He is not responding to you. Do you feel like He has gone MIA? Does it seem like you keep getting handed difficult things to overcome, repeatedly, without seeing His intervention? Or, that He overlooked the desires of your heart, and you will have to figure out how to move on? Are you wrestling with a feeling of being abandoned by the Lord? Right now, at this moment, you feel forgotten by the Lord.

I have been there too, and the pain is real. Two words: BUT GOD. I am learning in my walk with the Lord that the truth is, God can never forget! God does not forget the call He placed on our lives. God does not forget the desires of our hearts that He placed in there. He has not forgotten that we are His children and, therefore, His responsibility. What happens is over time; when faced with difficult circumstances and delays, we get the impression that God has most certainly forgotten about us. It is easy to assume that God has abandoned us when we are in the middle of something hard, and He seems to be silent. BUT the truth is, God cannot forget! He is Omniscient, and He knows all things. Beloved, God is still with you in the thick of all the mess. He sees you right now where you are, and He is working all things together for your good and His glory. (Romans 8:28)

We can find comfort in our key verse, knowing that God remembers us, and His lovingkindness towards us is everlasting. When we read in the Bible that God "remembered" something, it is not implying forgetfulness. It is an anthropomorphism, God merely speaking as if He were a man.

God always remembers—it is part of His nature.

The statement that "God remembered" actually places emphasis on His faithfulness and everlasting care toward us. When we go back to His Word and dig a little deeper, we can be encouraged by what we see when God remembers a person or group of people.

"God was faithful to Noah before the flood and after the flood. God remembered Noah and all the wild animals and the livestock that were with him in the ark." (Genesis 8:1)

"For years, Hannah wept and petitioned the Lord to conceive a child. Early the next morning, they arose and worshiped before the LORD and then went back to their home at Ramah. Elkanah made love to his wife, Hannah, and the LORD remembered her." (1 Samuel 1:19)

"God heard Rachel's desperation to give Jacob children. Then God remembered Rachel, and God listened to her and opened her womb." (Genesis 30:22)

"Abraham stood still before the Lord petitioning Him to spare the righteous from the destruction of Sodom. Thus it came about, when God destroyed the cities of the valley, that God remembered Abraham, and sent Lot out of the midst of the overthrow when He overthrew the cities in which Lot lived." (Genesis 19:29)

The Israelites would not be defined by their slavery, but by their convenient relationship with God, who heard their cries and who saw their affliction. During those many days, the king of Egypt died, and the people of Israel groaned because of their slavery and cried out for help. Their cry for rescue from slavery came up to God. And God heard their groaning, and God remembered His covenant with Abraham, with Isaac, and with Jacob. God saw the people of Israel—and God knew. (Exodus 2:23-24)

We can continue to wait earnestly with hope for He will remember. God will show his lovingkindness and faithfulness towards us. Because God is who He says He is. God will perform the word He has spoken over your life in His perfect timing. Because God will do what He said He would do. You can rest in knowing that nothing you could do, or have done, changes the love of the Father toward you. Because you are who God says you are. Find some time to get quiet and remind the Lord of the Promises He spoke over your life. I like what James Boice says, "The hope is not in reasoning that God is aware of all things and is therefore aware of you. That is true, but not always helpful. The hope is in knowing that God will act again! And in the meantime, your job is to go on in faithful obedience to what He has already shown you — however long ago that may have been." Let us ask the Lord to remember us. To act again on our behalf! He is ever faithful, and He will show us His lovingkindness again. We must do as Paul charged Timothy and remember the prophecies previously made concerning us that by them, we may wage the good warfare. (1 Timothy 1:18)

God is not overwhelmed with our requests.

He is not a God that cannot handle our persistent prayers. God does not get flustered in hearing His children petition the throne of grace. God knows you by name. He knows the very number of hairs on your head.

(Luke 12:7) As children of God, we are beneficiaries of the Promises He has made, and in Him, they are yes and amen. (2 Corinthians 1:20)

"Remember me, O Lord, with the favor You have toward Your people; Oh, visit me with Your salvation. Remember your word to your servant, for you have given me hope. My comfort in my suffering is this: Your promise preserves my life." (Psalms 106:4, Psalm 119:49-50)

A Closer Walk With Jesus

JOURNAL/REFLECTIONS

1. Have you ever felt like the Lord has not heard your prayers?

_____
_____
_____
_____
_____
_____
_____
_____
_____

2. How has God remembered you like He did with Noah, Rachel, Hannah, and the Israelites?

_____
_____
_____
_____
_____
_____
_____
_____
_____
_____
_____
_____
_____

3. What are promises God has spoken over you that you need to recall and refresh hope that God will remember?

Personal Prayer

JESUS WAS REJECTED

"You were bought at a price; do not become slaves of men." (1 Corinthians 7:23)

I was scrolling through social media, and there it is… pictures of a close friend's birthday celebration that I was not invited to attend. I scrolled down further, and I see photos of a business brunch with members of my team I also did not receive an invitation to join. Immediately, all these thoughts start running through my mind. "Wow, that looked like fun." "Hmmm, wonder why I wasn't invited?" "Why didn't she tell me she was having a birthday celebration?" "Am I not good enough?" "Is it because I am married and have kids?" "Does she enjoy that friend's husband more than mine?" "Wonder why they didn't include me in the business outing, I mean I am a part of the team?" The thoughts went on and on. And, before I knew it, the lies were formed, and I had bought them all, hook, line, and sinker.

The reality is rejection comes in all shapes and sizes. It can look like not getting your parent's approval. Someone else got the promotion you were seeking. You did not receive an invitation to the event you desired to be asked to attend. Your group of friends did not include you again. A spouse came home and said they were leaving. A friend suddenly blindsides you with betrayal. A child turns their back on your love for them. Your gifts and talents are not received well with certain people you do life with on a regular basis.

There is no doubt that rejection is painful, and it is a certainty. We will all face rejection at some point in our lifetime.

The word *rejection* comes from a Latin word that means "to be thrown back." When we experience rejection, the feeling not only stops us in our present pursuits, but it sometimes causes us to retreat from progressing, because we fear future failure. In psychology, this phenomenon is called *learned helplessness*. We are most vulnerable at the point of rejection. We experience disapproval or repudiation, and that experience becomes a catalyst for self-defeat. We can tend to internalize all the times we have been rejected and allowed lies of rejection to infiltrate our thoughts. So, every time we start to move forward in the areas we have experienced rejection, the fear within us affirms the lies we have believed about ourselves. We cannot afford to sit in a place of rejection. Because what happens is, we begin to view all interactions with others and circumstances through the lens of that rejection and pain. Our view becomes distorted, and our responses follow. I love what Lisa Terkeurst says in her book *Uninvited*[i], "Rejection steals the best of who I am by reinforcing the worse of what's been said to me." If we give this rejection the power to define us, it will always haunt us. On the contrary, if we allow rejection the capability to refine us, then that hurt will give way to healing.

We can look at the life of Jesus and take comfort in knowing He, too, experienced the pain of rejection.

Family rejected Jesus.

His own family rejected the call placed on his life, for even His brothers did not believe in Him. Then, Jesus said to them, "My time has not yet come, but your time is always ready. The world cannot hate you, but it hates Me because I testify of it that its works are evil." (John 7:5-7)

A Closer Walk With Jesus

Friends rejected Jesus.

Jesus knew what rejection from a close friend felt like. I imagine Jesus and Peter were quite the friends. They probably had many conversations, laughed together, ate together, celebrated together, and prayed together. This remarkably close friend of Jesus betrayed Him in a very crucial moment. "Certainly, this man also was with him, for he too is a Galilean." But Peter said, "Man, I do not know what you are talking about." And immediately, while he was still speaking, the rooster crowed. And the Lord turned and looked at Peter. And Peter remembered the saying of the Lord, how he had said to him, "Before the rooster crows today, you will deny me three times." And he went out and wept bitterly." (Luke 22:59-62)

The community rejected Jesus.

I would suggest Jesus, well known in His community, was a man with a reputation. The community loved and respected His parents, and He is despised and rejected by men, a Man of sorrows, and acquainted with grief. And we hid, as it were, our faces from Him; He was despised, and we did not esteem Him. (Isaiah 53:3) He came to His own, and His own did not receive Him. (John 1:11)

So, what can we gather from the rejection that Jesus faced? We know that Jesus knew His father loved Him and accepted Him. As you come to Him, the living stone rejected by humans, but chosen by God and precious to Him. (1 Peter 2:4) Jesus understood the call placed on His life and did not allow the pain of rejection to detour Him from the assignment at hand. Jesus, knowing that the Father had given all things into His hands and that He had come from God and was going to God. (John 13:3) If we are going to be over-comers of the pain of rejection, like Jesus, we need to understand who we are in Father. We need a revelation of the love that God has for us! We must know God has placed a call on our lives for His glory and the advancement of the Kingdom. Like Jesus, despite the pain of rejection, we need to be purposed to be about the Father's business. (John 5:19) We must renew our minds with the washing of God's Word to bring us freedom from the pain of rejection. (Romans 12:2) When we have experienced rejection, we must replace the lie with God's truth. For example, when I was scrolling through social media and saw I did not get an invitation to a close friend's birthday celebration, the lie I believed was, "I'm not accepted." The truth is, "I am accepted in the beloved." (Ephesians 1:5-6)

Our key verse offers us freedom and hope when it comes to rejection. Beloved, the beautiful truth is this; we have been bought for a price. That price was the blood of Jesus. Whatever rejection we have faced, or will face, God can heal if we will let Him.

The blood of Jesus will always speak a better word. (Hebrews 12:24)

We have been redeemed from rejection through the blood of Jesus. We have been chosen in love and accepted by the Father.

"Blessed are you when men hate you, And when they exclude you, And revile you, and cast out your name as evil, For the Son of Man's sake. Rejoice in that day and leap for joy! For indeed, your reward is great in heaven." (Luke 6:22-23a)

JOURNAL/REFLECTIONS

1. How has rejection affected you?

___

2. When looking at the life of Jesus, how can you take comfort in knowing He understands the pain that rejection has caused you?

___

3. Romans 12:2, Hebrews 12:24, 1 Corinthians 7:23, how do these verses give you hope in overcoming rejection?

Personal Prayer

HEAVENLY EXCHANGE

"Can any one of you by worrying add a single hour to your life?" (Matthew 6:27)

Turn your eyes upon Jesus, look firm in His wonderful face, and the weight of this world will grow strangely dim in the light of His glory and grace. She sang that song to me as I sat in her arms, bawling like a baby. I was on my second mission's trip over in Cambodia, living in an orphanage. I had come down with some sort of bacterial infection, causing open sores that were infected pretty severely, covering my legs and arms. They itched uncontrollably, and the pain was almost unbearable. I could not get the proper care I needed or the medication. All these questions began to swirl in my head. Fear and worry had overtaken me, and I pondered the scariest question of all, what if I died over here?

Did you know Jesus commands us, "Do not worry about your life, what you will eat or drink; or about your body, what you will wear. Is not life more than food and the body more than clothes?" (Matthew 6:25-27) We do not have to be anxious about anything, but in everything by prayer and supplication with thanksgiving, let our requests be made known to our Father. (Philippians 4:6-7) Being afraid or worrying about life's circumstances or current situations reveals a heart issue, we need God to deal with in us. At the root of it all, we do not trust God enough to handle whatever it is we are worried about. We need to allow God to bring us to a place where we believe that He is good all the time, no matter what the outcome is we face. He is the solution to every problem we have. Our Heavenly Father is for us, not against us. (Romans 8:31) His thoughts towards us are lovely. He delights over us with singing and dancing (Zephaniah 3:17). Nothing we are going through, or will ever go through, catches Him by surprise. (Isaiah 46:10) We have to move passed the head knowledge and believe deep within our hearts that with Him, all things are truly possible. (Matthew 19:26) He is God of all mankind. Is there anything too hard for Him? (Jeremiah 32:27) When we meditate and believe in these truths, we can wage war with worry and be victorious!

Our key verse is a hard truth to swallow. A truth we must hear to bring us back to the feet of Jesus. Worrying has nothing beneficial to offer us. God knows the enemy will use worry to decrease our hope and limit our victories. Therefore, when life gets messy and we find ourselves worrying, we need to make a heavenly exchange. We cast all our anxiety on Him because He cares for us (1 Peter 5:7), and in exchange, we get His peace. We come giving Him our labor and heavy load, and in exchange, we receive His rest. (Matthew 11:28-30) We give Him our weakness; in exchange, He gives us His strength. (Philippians 4:13, Romans 8:26-28)

I decided that afternoon that I was going to worship through my worrying and go to the throne room. I put worship music on my iPod and went for a walk into the marketplace. The Holy Spirit led me into a shop where He told me to purchase a bracelet. I was not sure why, but being obedient, I did. I will never forget as I was walking out, the song by David Crowder was playing, "Oh How He Loves Us.[iii]"

I was a sobbing mess. I immediately heard the Holy Spirit tell me to look to my right. When I did, underneath the very basket of bracelets like the one I had purchased, was an oversized piece of posterboard with some English writing that caught my attention. I scrambled to move the basket and uncover the posterboard. On it was written:

"I have heard your prayer and seen your tears; I will heal you." (2 Kings 20:5)

God sent His Word and healed me. He healed my physical body, but at that moment, He also set me free from worry, fear, and anxiety. That bracelet I bought was a reminder to me that a heavenly exchange was made. When I decided to surrender my worry about this situation to Him, He sent His Word and healed me. Within twenty-four hours, my wounds were scabbing and healing. All Glory to God!

When circumstances start to overwhelm us, we must turn our eyes to Jesus, just like the lyrics to Helen Howarth Lemmel's song suggests. As we learn not give in to the temptation to worry and instead make a heavenly exchange, our testimony will be like the Psalmist David's, "I sought the LORD, and he answered me and delivered me from all of my fears." (Psalm 34:4)

JOURNAL/REFLECTIONS

1. What affect does worry, or anxiety, have on your life?

_____
_____
_____
_____
_____
_____
_____
_____
_____

2. How can you wage war on worry or anxiety?

_____
_____
_____
_____
_____
_____
_____
_____
_____
_____
_____
_____
_____

3. What are some Scriptures you can memorize, or place around your house, to remind you not to worry or be anxious?

_____
_____
_____
_____
_____
_____
_____
_____
_____
_____
_____

Personal Prayer

_____
_____
_____
_____
_____
_____
_____
_____
_____
_____
_____
_____
_____
_____
_____
_____

NEVER THE SAME

"I have heard of You by the hearing of the ear, But now my eye sees You." (Job 42:5)

I found myself in a cold jail cell, all alone. I had way too much to drink and passed out at the wheel. My car ran out of gas in the middle of the interstate, and that is where the state trooper found me. A local school happened to be visiting the jail for a field trip that day. As the kids toured the prison, they saw me locked up. Me, the one who loves kids, I was absolutely horrified and humiliated. I had hit rock bottom and knew that if something did not change, this life I was living, would result in my death. I remember thinking that night in the jail cell, "If you are real God, I need You to show up now." As I faced the truth of my situation, I reflected on how my life was full of disappointment, rejection, fear, addiction, hopelessness, confusion, and worry. I had sought after the things of this world to fill a void that only Jesus could fill. I was in shackles to a depraved mind and lies.

February 14th, 2009, Jesus met me in that cold cell, and I have never been the same since.

This one encounter with Jesus, everything changed. Jesus took me by the hand and led me out of my addiction, out of my bondage, and into my freedom in Him!

As children of faith, we need to regularly have face to face encounters with Jesus. One encounter with Jesus and our situation is changed. Our hearts are changed. Our character is changed. Every time we have an encounter with Jesus, we are transformed from glory to glory. (2 Corinthians 3:18) Our encounters with Jesus speak to our sphere of influence that there is something more significant to seek after than what the world has offered. As we have encounters with Jesus and testify of His goodness, we are giving others an invitation to seek Jesus for their encounter with Him, as well. Like Job, in our key verse, here are a few men and women that have the same testimony of encountering the Living God and everything changing in their lives.

The woman who bled for twelve years had suffered a great deal under the care of many doctors and had spent all she had, yet instead of getting better, she grew worse. In her day, she was legally rendered unclean. She has one encounter with Jesus, and at that moment, her bleeding stopped. Health restored to her body instantly. The unclean woman had been made clean. (Luke 8:43-48)

Saul, who is a Roman citizen, a zealot for Judaism, and Pharisee with a renowned reputation of persecuting and killing Christians, has one encounter with Jesus, transforming him forever. He would be used for church planting and spreading the Gospel message of forgiveness. He was a missionary to the Gentiles. Preaching with signs and wonders following. (Acts 9:1-22)

The woman at the well, known for her multiple husbands, an outcast and hated Samaritan woman has an encounter with Jesus, becoming an heir of God, introducing her neighbors to the Savior of the World. (John 4:4-42)

A Closer Walk With Jesus

Lazarus, sick unto to death, has one encounter with Jesus, and his lifeless body, wrapped in grave clothes, was resurrected from the dead. (John 11:1-44)

Billy Graham has one encounter with Jesus, over seventy years ago, in a hotel room in Los Angeles, California transforming him into one of the Church's all-time great evangelists who ushered hundreds of thousands of souls into the Kingdom of God.

Dwight L. Moody has one encounter with Jesus during a prayer meeting in a hayfield that took him from a poorly educated, unconfident shoe salesman into one of the greatest evangelists of modern times. He preached revivals across England and the United States, where tens of thousands came to know Christ as Savior.

Have you found yourself in a dry place, feeling defeated, overwhelmed, confused, frustrated, and exhausted? Maybe like me, you have looked in all the wrong places for the solution to the problems you are facing? I want to encourage you beloved that Jesus has the answer.

Jesus is the answer.

He is ready to have a love encounter with you. Seek Him, and you will find Him. You will never be the same. One encounter with Him and He will refresh you, restore you, and heal you. Let us be children of faith who come near to God, and He will come near to us.

JOURNAL/REFLECTIONS

1. When and how did you first meet Jesus?

___

2. What was your most recent encounter with Jesus?

___

3. Out of the examples given of the men and women, which one do you relate to the most and why?

_____
_____
_____
_____
_____
_____
_____
_____

Personal Prayer

_____
_____
_____
_____
_____
_____
_____
_____
_____
_____
_____
_____
_____

A NEW THING

"Do not remember the former things, nor consider the things of old. Behold, I will do a new thing, now it shall spring forth; Shall you not know it?" (Isaiah 43:18-19a)

As you enter a new year, it is often a time again where a lot of us take the opportunity set before us to examine our lives over the last 365 days and to make resolutions to do some things differently moving forward.

Many see the new year as a chance to wipe the slate clean and start fresh. For some, it looks like changing the way they eat to live a healthier lifestyle. Others, it is getting into a daily routine of exercise. There will be those that determine that in this new year, they want to live their lives with more purpose. Maybe for you, it is learning to budget and manage money better. Speaking of resolutions, did you know that according to a study conducted by the University of Scranton, just 8 percent of people achieve their New Year's goals.

In comparison, around 80 percent fail to keep their New Year's resolutions, says US clinical psychologist Joseph Luciani. Those statistics are shocking! Resolutions are a great idea; however, what we need is God's wisdom and vision regarding what He wants to accomplish in and through our lives in the New Year. We must want our desires to align with God's desires, and then we can freely receive His grace to walk in obedience to see them fulfilled.

So, as you reflect on this year, maybe it was a challenging one for you. It has been a year that has you questioning a lot of things. Does it seem like a year of events that have caused a lot of pain, stress, and grief? Or for some, it might have been an utterly fantastic year! A year of celebrations and incredible achievements. Our key verse offers us wisdom and hope as we continue to push through this year. We are instructed in God's Word not to dwell on the past, to forget about what has happened, and not to keep going over old history. (Isaiah 43:18-19) If we have wounds from the past we have not dealt with, let us bring them now before the Lord and receive healing, so that we can move forward in freedom. (1 John 1:9, Psalm 119:45) If there is anything that has caused ungodly fruit to come forth from our lives, may we go boldly before the throne of grace, allowing God to deal with those matters graciously. (Hebrews 4:16)

No matter how great or horrible our past might have been, we have to choose to live our lives, not looking back. For no one who puts his hand to the plow and looks back is fit for the Kingdom of God. (Luke 9:62) When we live our lives in a state of looking back, it causes us to go off course. If we are living in a constant place of past regret, pain, disappointments, and the frustration of unmet expectations, it keeps us in bondage unable to live in the present fully. God wants us to come to Him and to receive healing and live a life of freedom, receiving fully all the blessings He has for us right now.

Isaiah 43, verse 19, encourages us to be present and alert.

Jesus was the perfect example of living this lifestyle. John 5:19 tells us that Jesus was always about His Father's business. When God spoke, Jesus moved. We, too, must be sober-minded and watchful, so that we do not miss what the Lord is doing. (1 Peter 5:8-9)

A Closer Walk With Jesus

Our key verse ends with the Lord saying, "I'm about to do something brand-new. It's bursting out! Don't you see it?" To see the new thing God is doing, we have to be willing to embrace change. Jesus cannot put new wine into old wineskins. If He does, the wine will burst the skins, and the wine is destroyed, and so are the skins. We need new wineskins to hold the new wine He is pouring out in this new era. (Mark 2:22) Let us not miss what God is doing right now, because we lack vision and wisdom.

The Bible clearly warns us that where there is no vision, the people perish. (Proverbs 29:18) If any of us lacks wisdom, we should ask God, who gives generously to all without finding fault, and it will be given to us. (James 1:5) This wisdom that comes from Heaven is first of all pure; then peace-loving, considerate, submissive, full of mercy and good fruit, impartial and sincere. (James 3:17) It is crucial as believers; we get God's vision and wisdom for our lives, even as we move through this year. God is waiting for you and me to come, sit, and listen, so He can reveal His secrets to us. (Psalm 25:14) He has plans to prosper us. (Jeremiah 29:11) Let this be the year we trust fully in the Lord with all our hearts and not lean on our own understanding. (Proverbs 3:5-6) Let us be intentional about getting still and knowing that He is God. May we seek the Lord for He gives wisdom; from His mouth come knowledge and understanding. (Psalm 46:10, Proverbs 2:6)

When this present year has come to an end, may we see that our lives produced godly fruit for the glory of God. (John 15:8) Let our testimony be that we sought the Lord, did not remember the former things, continued to be alert, and we have tasted and seen the goodness of the Lord. (Psalm 34:8)

JOURNAL/REFLECTIONS

1. Why does Scripture tell us not to consider the former things, or to dwell on the past?

_____
_____
_____
_____
_____
_____
_____
_____
_____
_____

2. What is the importance of having new wineskins? (Mark 2:22)

_____
_____
_____
_____
_____
_____
_____
_____
_____
_____
_____
_____
_____
_____

3. Proverbs 29:18 states that we perish for a lack of vision. Why is it important to have vision? What is the vision God has given you for this year?

_____
_____
_____
_____
_____
_____
_____
_____
_____
_____

Personal Prayer

_____
_____
_____
_____
_____
_____
_____
_____
_____
_____
_____
_____
_____
_____

FOLLOW THE INSTRUCTION

"Jesus came to him and said, 'Launch your net on the other side.'" And when they had done this, they caught a great number of fish, and their net was breaking. So they signaled to their partners in the other boat to come and help them. And they came and filled both the boats so that they began to sink." (Luke 5:4-5)

According to the Oxford dictionary, the definition of *instruction* is detailed information telling how something should be done, operated, or assembled.

Recently, my youngest son Zeph has discovered the stairs in our house, which has caused us to purchase a baby gate to protect him from falling down them! Now, you would think a baby gate should only take a few minutes to install. Let me say, in our case, that was not so. It took three of us, some power tools, and about two hours. I know you are wondering why in the world did it take that many people and that long? Ha! Well, because we did not follow the instructions that were given. After installing and uninstalling quite a few times, we finally got it. All we had to do from the beginning to avoid the time wasted, frustration, and exhaustion was to follow the simple instructions.

I want to suggest that miracles are often birthed by following instructions through obedience in faith.

Let me be the first to tell you we serve a God that is still in the miracle-working business. (Matthew 19:26) He is the same yesterday, today, and forever. (Hebrews 13:8) I speak from a place where I know this to be fully accurate. My husband and I have received some pretty radical miracles from financial miracles to healing miracles and everything in between!

Oxford dictionary defines a *miracle* as a surprising and welcomed event that is not explicable by natural or scientific laws and is therefore considered the work of a divine agency.

Our miracles often require us to be obedient to God's voice. We must start listening for the instruction of the Lord and obey in faith without hesitation. As children of God, we hear the voice of our Shepherd and do not follow the voice of another. (John 10:27) Stay with me here and let us take a look at a few miracles in the Word of God where instructions were given, obedience followed, and miracles were birthed.

His first miracle, Jesus revealed His glory to His disciples by coming to the rescue at a wedding in Cana in Galilee when there became a wine shortage. The instruction: to fill the vases with water and pour it into the guest's glasses. Miracle: The water poured into the glasses became wine. (John 2:7-9)

Jesus is feeding the multitude to show His love and compassion further miraculously; on two occasions, Jesus fed thousands of His admirers from merely a few loaves of bread and fish that were gathered by his disciples. Instruction: Bring the five loaves and two fish to me. Miracle: He blessed and broke and gave the loaves to the disciples, and the disciples gave to the multitudes. So they all ate and were filled, and they took up twelve baskets full of the fragments that remained. (Matthew 14:19-20)

The Lord had given Jericho into the hands of Joshua, but first, he had to follow the instruction. Instruction: March around the walls one time for six days, and on the 7th day, you shall blow the trumpets and shout with a great shout, and the walls will come down. Miracle: And it happened when the people heard the sound of the trumpet, and the people shouted with a great shout, that the wall fell flat. Then the people went up into the city, every man straight before him, and they took the city. (Joshua 6)

The Levitical priests were given instruction: to take the Ark of the Covenant and to carry it into the waters of Jordan. Miracle: And it shall come to pass, as soon as the soles of the feet of the priests who bear the ark of the Lord, the Lord of all the earth, shall rest in the waters of the Jordan, that the waters of the Jordan shall be cut off, the waters that come down from upstream, and they shall stand as a heap. (Joshua 3)

The widow who needed provision and food. Instruction: Then he said, "Go, borrow vessels from everywhere, from all your neighbors—empty vessels; do not gather just a few. And when you have come in, you shall shut the door behind you and your sons; then pour it into all those vessels, and set aside the full ones." Miracle: God multiplied the oil! She was able to pay off her debt, and she and her sons lived off the rest. (2 Kings 4)

A man born blind. When Jesus had said these things, He spat on the ground and made clay with the saliva, and He anointed the eyes of the blind man with the clay. Instruction: He said to him, "Go, wash in the pool of Siloam." So, he went and washed. Miracle: He came back with his sight. (John 9:6-7)

Oh, how we are contending for miracles, but we do not want to follow instructions and be obedient through faith. (James 2) How many times has God wanted to perform miracles on our behalf, but we weren't willing to follow the instruction? We are afraid of what people might think if we did what the Lord had asked of us. Or we think to ourselves, "Surely that wasn't God asking me to do that?" How many of us have missed financial miracles because we have refused to heed the instruction of the Lord on tithing, alms, and giving, finding ourselves barely getting by, or on the brink of bankruptcy? (Malachi 3:8-10) How many parents have not heeded the uncompromising instructions from the book of Proverbs on child-rearing and have not seen their miracle of having a God-fearing, pure, praying, child?

Our key verse shows us how following a simple instruction can bring such a blessing not only to us, but to those around us! They were tired and had strived all night to catch a single fish and came up short. Yet, in a moment the Lord spoke, they obeyed, and now their boat was sinking with blessing!

Listen, beloved; nothing is too hard for the Lord. (Jeremiah 32:27) Whatever miracle you are pressing in for, He can perform it! Do not lose heart in the waiting.

Follow the instruction and wait with expectation for Him to do immeasurably more than you have asked or imagined. (Ephesians 3:20)

Miracles happen when God moves. Blind eyes are opened. (John 9) The deaf begin to hear. The dead are raised to life. The lame begin to walk. (Matthew 11:5) Strongholds are broken. (2 Corinthians 10:4) He is the Lord, and He does not change. (Malachi 3:6) God is no respecter of people. What He does for one of His children, He will do for another. (Romans 2:11) Everything is possible to him who believes. (Mark 9:23) We must put our faith into action and be obedient when He speaks. When the instruction is given, act. Your testimony will be that like Job's: God performs wonders that cannot be fathomed, miracles that cannot be counted. (Job 5:8)

A Closer Walk With Jesus

Father God, thank You that You are still in the business of performing miracles today. Please help us to listen for the instruction that will bring forth our miracle. We declare our testimony will be Deuteronomy 10:21, impressive wonders we see with our own eyes. We love You, Lord, and thank You by faith for our miracle. In Jesus' name, Amen.

JOURNAL/REFLECTIONS

1. What miracle are you needing God to perform?

_____
_____
_____
_____
_____
_____
_____
_____
_____
_____

2. What is the instruction the Lord has given you to see your miracle come to pass?

_____
_____
_____
_____
_____
_____
_____
_____
_____
_____
_____
_____
_____
_____

3. Is there something holding you back from receiving your miracle? If so, what is it?

___

Personal Prayer

___

JUST KEEP WALKING

"Yea though I walk through the valley of the shadow of death, I will fear no evil; For you are with me; for your rod and staff, they comfort me." (Psalm 23:4)

I have come to realize that in this life, we will experience valleys. We will face many trials and tribulations. The truth about valleys is they are always subject to change. We should find it pure joy when we fall into various trials, because of the work that is happening within us. (James 1:1-2) Submitting to the work of the Lord amidst the valleys causes our faith to be authentic. Sometimes, we suffer grief or joy in all kinds of trials. These trials have come, so that our faith will be greater than gold. (1 Peter 1:6-7) This kind of faith will result in praise and glory to Christ.

The valleys we walk through will produce an aroma that is satisfying to the Lord.

Through tribulations, God uses them to perfect His purpose in us and through us. Suffering has a way of making us real and brings glory to God. These valleys have a way of making us merely beautiful.

Beloved, our trials have great purpose, even in the midst of great pain.

They can teach us how to walk out the Word of God we confess to believe. Our valleys can be places where the rubber meets the road, causing us to put our faith into action. The Lord will use our valleys to teach us things beneficial for our growth and development of character if we are willing to trust Him through the pain of what we endure.

Our key verse says, "Yea though I walk through the valley of the shadow of death, I will fear no evil; for you are with me; for your rod and staff, they comfort me." The word "walk" indicates the steady advance of one which knows its road, identifies its end, resolves to follow the path, feels safe, and is therefore perfectly calm and composed. You see, we have to walk through the valleys. Despite the intense pain or the fear of the unknown, we have an opportunity set before us to trust God and walk through it. Allowing God full range to use what we are walking through for our good and His glory. (Romans 8:28)

We must then trust our Shepherd's care, and hearken to His voice.

The enemy would love for us to buy the lies that say we cannot bear to walk through this trial. He will bait us with fear, lies, and confusion to get us to do anything but walk. The Word of God does not tell us to settle in the valley and give up. It does not say, "Hey, you won't survive this trial, so go ahead and turn around." No, it does not. It does not mean that we are to pitch a tent and camp out in the hardship. Quite the contrary! The Living Word of God tells us to "walk." That is it, friend. Yes, just one step at a time.

It is surrendering to God one foot in front of the other, as He leads us through the mess of it all.

Do you know why we can walk through the valley of the shadow of death? Because God is with us. He is there through it all, ready to comfort us. God will not leave us in the middle of the valley. He sees us right where we are and is holding on to our hearts, as we walk through it all. This reminds me of a woman named Hagar in the Old Testament. She was a woman who understood that we serve a God who *sees*. (Genesis 16:13)

God gave us Scripture to spark our faith, provide us with life, and equip us for everything we would go through. (1 Timothy 3:16-17) His Word is a weapon that helps us to overcome. Like Paul, I do not consider myself yet to lay hold of it. But one thing I do: forgetting what is behind and pressing on toward the goal to win the prize. (Philippians 3:13-14) We must keep a Kingdom perspective to walk through the trial victoriously. We can walk this thing out if we are trusting the One who is in it with us. God shapes us for the great purposes for which He has created us. He has created you, all your gifts, all your talents, all your valleys, all your hills, all your mountaintops, and moments of descent. Ephesians 2:10 says, "For we are His workmanship, created in Him to do good works, which God prepared beforehand so that we would walk in them."

Today, if you find yourself in a valley, I encourage you to do one thing, just… keep…walking!

JOURNAL/REFLECTIONS

1. What was the most recent valley you had to walk through?

2. Why is it important to walk through the valley?

3. How can you use the Word as a weapon to spark faith and overcome the valley?

Personal Prayer

<u>GIVE AND IT WILL BE GIVEN TO YOU</u>

"Give, and it will be given to you: good measure, pressed down, shaken together, and running over will be put int your bosom. For with the same measure that you use, it will be measured back to you." (Luke 6:38)

Give and it will be given to you. My wife and I have experienced this in our own lives more than we can recount. I remember one specific time we saw this that has marked me. It was a time God had told us to give a financial donation to help a widowed woman in need. A few days later, God paid off thousands of dollars of our medical debt through an acquaintance of mine's church!

Let us now look at three examples of giving and receiving from the scriptures.

1. John Chapter 6 tells of a great multitude of people who came out to see Jesus. Jesus would soon feed them all by performing a great miracle. Andrew said to Jesus the following in John 6:9: "There is a lad here who has five barley loaves and two small fish, but what are they among so many?"

John 6:10-11 says, "Then Jesus said, "Make the people sit down." Now there was much grass in the place. So the men sat down, in number about five thousand. And Jesus took the loaves, and when He had given thanks, He distributed them to the disciples, and the disciples to those sitting down; and likewise of the fish, as much as they wanted.

This boy did not come empty-handed before the Lord. He had something to give Jesus. It was not much, but it was something. He gave his meal to Jesus. How beautiful. The Lord accepted this humble sacrifice. He gave thanks and then distributed it to the disciples who then gave to the people. Jesus multiplied it! The people had as much as they wanted. After the people were filled, the disciples filled twelve baskets with the fragments of the five barley loaves, which were left over by those who had eaten.

That boy never missed a meal! He gave to Jesus and it was given back to him. He ate as much as he wanted, along with the people and they still had leftovers. When we give to Jesus, even the little things, He has a way of receiving what we give Him, and blessing it to such a degree, that He makes the end result of the gift greater than what was originally given.

2. 1 Kings 10:10 says, "Then she gave the king one hundred and twenty talents of gold, spices in great quantity, and precious stones. There never again came such abundance of spices as the queen of Sheba gave to King Solomon."

In this 2nd example from scripture, King Solomon is an Old Testament foreshadow of Jesus Christ who is the King of Kings. (Revelations 17:14) The Queen of Sheba brings a great gift to him of gold, spices, and precious stones. There never again came such abundance of spices as she gave to him. What a sacrifice she made! But wait, read how she is rewarded for such a generous gift three verses later!

1 Kings 10:13 says, "Now King Solomon gave the queen of Sheba all she desired, whatever she asked, besides what Solomon had given her according to the royal generosity. So she turned and went to her own country, she and her servants."

A Closer Walk With Jesus

Thank You Jesus for such encouragement from Your Word. She gave, and it was given back to her. Her spices did not own her. Her gold and precious stones did not own her. She gave them away and in return, received all she desired, everything she asked! Sometimes, the very thing that we are holding onto is the very thing we need to give away before we experience breakthrough in our lives.

Jesus is greater than Solomon. (Matthew 12:42) What is it that you seek from the Lord? Jesus is the answer, and He has the answers. He is salvation. He heals, delivers, provides, protects, and loves. He is peace. He is everything. If you yield your life to Him, you will not be disappointed. The more you give of your life to Him, the more He can accomplish in and through you for His glory!

There are many ways to give to Jesus. We can give Him our hearts, dreams, and ambitions. We can give Him our strength and health by working hard and helping others. We can give Him our time, money, and our praise. The list is endless. Giving to God is a beautiful thing. The boy brought 5 loaves of barley bread and 2 fishes and Jesus took them and fed 5,000 men. The Queen of Sheba brought gifts to Solomon and in return, got everything she desired, everything she asked.

Ephesians 3:20-21 says, "Now to Him who is able to do exceedingly abundantly above all that we ask or think, according to the power that works in us, to Him be glory in the church by Christ Jesus to all generations, forever and ever. Amen."

3. Let us close with one more example from Scripture about giving and receiving. John 3:16 says, "For God so loved the world that He gave His only begotten Son, that whoever believes in Him should not perish but have everlasting life."

God gave. He gave His best! He sacrificed His only begotten Son on the Cross, resulting in the salvation of many, of whoever believes in Jesus. God gave His Son in death and received His Son back to life again by His resurrection. In the process, God the Father was also bringing many sons to glory (Hebrews 2:10) through Jesus by adoption. (Galatians 4:5) That one act of giving His only begotten Son, resulted in Him gaining many sons, as well as Jesus back to Himself! So, God Himself fulfilled our opening verse of Luke 6:38 which says, "Give, and it will be given to you: good measure, pressed down, shaken together, and running over will be put into your bosom, For with the same measure that you use, it will be measured back to you."

Father, thank You for all You have given us. Help us become greater givers for Your glory. Thank You for the many blessings which You have blessed us with. Thank You for Your love, grace, power, and goodness. Open our spiritual eyes to see You as You are. Melt away the hardness of our hearts with Your love and goodness. Reveal to each of us Your kindness and thoughts towards us. You are so good to us. Receive that which we give You and bless it for Your glory in Jesus' name, Amen.

A Closer Walk With Jesus

JOURNAL/REFLECTIONS

1. Was there a time where the Lord asked you to give something and in return, you saw Him give back to you more than what you gave?

_____
_____
_____
_____
_____
_____
_____
_____
_____
_____

2. The more you give of your life to Jesus, the more He can accomplish in and through you for His glory! What are some things right now that you can give to Him?

_____
_____
_____
_____
_____
_____
_____
_____
_____

3. How does it make you feel to know that God gave His BEST to you? He gave His Son, Jesus.

_____
_____
_____
_____
_____
_____
_____
_____
_____
_____

Personal Prayer

_____
_____
_____
_____
_____
_____
_____
_____
_____
_____
_____
_____
_____

CREATED TO PRAISE

"About midnight, Paul and Silas were praying and singing hymns to God, and the other prisoners were listening to them. Suddenly there was such a violent earthquake that the foundations of the prison were shaken. At once, all the prison doors flew open, and everyone's chains came loose." (Acts 16:25-26)

When a baby takes their first steps, parents praise them. A teacher praises their students. Fans praise their teams' victory. When we pass a test we have studied for, we praise. When we overcome our adversaries, we praise. When we get a promotion, we praise. When we achieve something great, we praise. A coach praises his team. You accomplish a goal you set for yourself, you praise. Everywhere we look, we can see the evidence of praise in action.

We were created to praise.

It is in our very nature to express warm approval or admiration! We were created to praise our Creator. (Psalm 47:6) God wants you to know you have been called to a life of glorifying Him. Isaiah 43:21 says, "the people whom I formed for myself that they might declare my praise." Our very life was created to sing a song of praise to God. God is looking for those who will open their mouth and praise Him in Spirit and in Truth. (John 4:23) We praise Him for His goodness. His steadfast love. His greatness. His strength. We praise Him for His mighty deeds. Praise Him according to His excellent greatness! (Psalm 150:2) We must be people to answer the call and praise God, who is worthy to be praised! (Psalm 135:1-

3) How good it is to sing praises to our God, how pleasant and fitting to praise Him! (Psalm 147:1) We have been instructed by the Living Word of God to give thanks in all circumstances for this is God's will for you in Christ Jesus. (1 Thessalonians 5:18)

Praise changes everything.

Have you ever had a bad day? Maybe you are like me, and you have days where you have an attitude that well, just downright stinks? Perhaps you are in a funk and need to shake it off? Great news, I have an answer! One word. Praise! In those moments, beloved you have to decide that no matter what is going on or how you "feel" that you are going to open your mouth and begin to praise God!

We cannot be a people led by our "feelings".

Feelings are fickle and they are subject to change. (Galatians 5:25) We need to settle it deep in our hearts that we were created to praise God no matter what. We have been called to a position of praise. (Psalm 35:28) Praise is one of the most powerful ways we can change our life! Praise changes everything. Praise moves the heart of God the Father. (Psalms 149:4, Psalm 69:31) Praise invokes God's Presence. (Psalm 22:3) Praise silences the devil. (Psalm 8:2) Praise breaks strongholds. Our praise is a weapon of warfare. (2 Chronicles 20:22) Praising God redirects our focus, and suddenly our perspective changes. Praising God shifts our atmosphere, our heart, and our attitude.

Praise takes us to a place of humility.

When we choose to praise God, it brings us to a place of humility. Our praise to God says we need You; we acknowledge You; we love You, we look to You, and we honor and stand in reverence of You.

When we praise God, it is our own way of intimately expressing to Him how much He means to us.

It causes our hearts to bow, realizing our need for Him. Praising God reminds us that He is in control. He is the solution to every problem we face. (Proverbs 3:5-6) As we enter His gates with thanksgiving, everything changes. (Psalm 100:4) Oh come, let us worship and bow down; let us kneel before the Lord, our Maker! (Psalm 95:6)

Praise gives you victory over the enemy.

Our key verse can give us great hope in understanding the power of praising God. Let us get some background into the story first! The magistrates ordered Paul and Silas to be stripped and beaten with rods. After they had been severely flogged, he put them in the inner cell and fastened their feet in the stocks. (Acts 16:22-24) I would imagine these men were sitting in a cold prison cell in a pool of their blood, as their flesh was torn open and hanging. The pain they must have been in at the moment physically, mentally, and emotionally, I cannot fathom. Surely, they had every opportunity to be angry and fearful at this moment. BUT the Word records that at about midnight, Paul and Silas were praying and singing hymns to God!!! They chose to pray and sing praises to God, instead. What happened next is nothing short of the miraculous. Suddenly, there was such a violent earthquake that the foundations of the prison were shaken. At once all the prison doors flew open, and everyone's chains came loose. (Acts 16:26) Because of their choice to pray and sing praises to God, the Philippian jailer and his whole household were saved! You see, when we choose to praise God, we get the victory over the enemy. We receive peace in exchange for fear, understanding in exchange for confusion, joy in exchange for heaviness, and victory in exchange for defeat!

Beloved, whether we find ourselves overwhelmed with burdens, worried about tomorrow, or loving life on the mountaintop, we can make a choice to praise God for who He is, and His promises over us are *yes* and *amen*. (2 Corinthians 1:20) We can praise Him that we have been blessed with the free gift of salvation and eternal life. We must make it a practice to praise God for His goodness and honor Him. Let us not forget we have been called to praise the One who created us, and He is worthy to be praised.

Father God, thank You. Thank You that You are my Redeemer, defender, healer, provider, and friend. Help me to remember that through my praise, You give me victory over the enemy, You produce the fruit of humility in me, and I am fulfilling the call You have placed on me. In Jesus', name, Amen.

Beloved, Rejoice in the Lord always. I will say it again: Rejoice! (Philippians 4:4)

A Closer Walk With Jesus

JOURNAL/REFLECTIONS

1. According to Acts 16:25, what were Paul and Silas doing in prison before the earthquake?

_____

_____

_____

_____

_____

_____

_____

_____

_____

2. How does our praise change things?

_____

_____

_____

_____

_____

_____

_____

_____

_____

_____

_____

_____

3. How can Philippians 4:4 become more of a reality in your life?

Personal Prayer

WORD VS. WORLD

"This is how God showed his Love among us: He sent his one and only Son into the world that we might live through him. This is Love: not that we loved God, but that he loved us and sent his Son as an atoning sacrifice for our sins." (John 4:9-10)

Take a minute and look around you; everyone is searching for love. People want to be loved. We were created by God to be loved and to love. I would agree with Dr. Kurt Smith Psy.D. LMFT, LPCC, AFC that most of us tend to use the feeling of love to determine the duration of a relationship or friendship. May I suggest that a lot of times, unfortunately, we rely on the feeling of love to determine how we will treat others. Is it possible that we allow the feeling of love to have more power over what we say and do than we should? The feeling of falling in love with something or someone is easy to do, almost effortless, but losing that loving feeling is not that hard to do, either. Feelings are fickle and are subject to change at a moment's notice. Suppose love was more than just a feeling. Instead of love solely being a feeling, what if it was a choice we had to make, that calls us to action?

The world says…

The world's definition of love is an intense feeling of deep affection. The world often suggests love is just a feeling, which is correct, but not in its entirety. The world also views love through a lens of perversion, which results in lust. The world's view tends to place limits on love according to gender, religion, status, and race. The world says since love is a feeling, we are to treat people according to the way someone makes us feel. The world says love someone because they are lovable. Love someone because they love what you love. Show love to someone because they give you that warm, fuzzy feeling. Do something in love because they love you in return. Is it challenging to show someone love when you have that feeling of love towards them? No, it is not even the Bible that says sinners show love to those who love them. (Luke 6:32) What does the world say to do when someone mistreats us? What is the world's solution to someone who repeatedly says hurtful things towards us?

That feeling of love we once had toward them becomes calloused. A person does not agree on the same topics of interest; therefore, my feeling of showing them love disappears. We will help those we love, we will even do favors for them, but those same people do something that hurts us, and in a moment, we decide we do not care to show love anymore towards them. They did not react the way we wanted them to. They did not show their gratitude toward us. They did not stick up for us when we thought they should have. They did not text or call us back. Whatever the case may be, we get offended, and the feeling to love them is now gone. Why? Because feelings are fleeting. Before we know it, we take the easy route out. We stop making the choice to love them, extending grace, forgiving them, and we simply move on. The world's idea of love is subject to change, and is self-centered and self-seeking.

The Word of God says…

The Word's definition says love is patient and kind; love does not envy or boast; it is not arrogant or rude. It does not insist on its own way; it is not irritable or resentful; it does not rejoice at wrongdoing, but rejoices with the truth. Love bears all things, believes all things, hopes all things, endures all things. Love never ends. (1 Corinthians 13:4-8) When we understand the true definition of love, there is a freedom to love no matter what. According to this scripture, when we use the word "love" toward someone, we must ask ourselves these questions. Am I being patient and kind? Am I rejoicing in truth? Am I enduring, believing, and hoping all things? Am I being humble? Am I keeping no record of wrong against this person? We have to get an understanding that unconditional love places no limits on the other person. It is selfless.

The highest call we have is to love God! (Matthew 22:37)

"The second is this: 'Love your neighbor as yourself.' There is no commandment greater than these." (Mark 12:31) We have been called to love those the world deems unlovable. (Luke 6:32-42) And then, there is the call to love our enemies, do good to those who hate us, bless those who curse us, and pray for those who mistreat us. (Luke 6:27) The Word goes on to say, "Above all, love each other deeply, because love covers over a multitude of sins." (1 Peter 4:8) "Be completely humble and gentle; be patient, bearing with one another in love." (Ephesians 4:2) "My command is this: love each other as I have loved you." (John 15:12) Love must be sincere. (Romans 12:9) A friend loves at all times. (Proverbs 17:17) We get the opportunity to be used by God to show the world what love looks like! We can choose to be kind and patient, whether we think someone deserves it or not.

Our key verse shows us that love is a choice. God chose to send His Son, Jesus, to die for us that we might be reconciled to Him. Love is a choice calling us into action. An invitation to show the world what it looks like to be patient and kind, not prideful or arrogant. God shows us His love for us through His actions. If God is kind to the ungrateful and the wicked, then so should we! (Luke 6:35) God deeply and affectionately loves you!

His Love for you is unconstrained—no strings attached, and there is nothing that you can do to separate you from God's love. (Romans 8:38-39) Before you can love others, you must receive God's love for yourself, because you cannot give away something you do not have.

God is patient and kind towards you. He sent His Son, Jesus to take your place on the Cross, bearing all your sins, so that your record of wrongdoing would be thrown into the sea of forgetfulness. His love for you came at the high price. Knowing that God loves you is central to your understanding of the Gospel, for the entire Gospel is based on God's love. God's love for us is not based on our works or our accomplishments. God does not ever fall out of love with us. Nothing you have done, whether great or horrific in the past or even now, could ever change the love that God has for us! God's love for us only grows deeper and more passionately toward us.

God's Love for us never ends.

What would our workplace, community, church, school, or neighborhood look like if we chose to be conduits of the same love God shows us? What would happen if we purposed in our hearts to live love out loud well? You see, one love encounter with God changes everything! You are never the same! God's love has the power to change anything in one moment. God wants to use us a vessel that His great love can flow through, bringing a shift to a lost and broken generation. We are not citizens of this world, but Heaven. We have been called to show God's love to those around us in its purest form. There is no expiration date on our call to love. There are no terms that ever call us to stop loving those around us. Let these words encourage you today to choose to love according to God's definition, not the worlds.

A Closer Walk With Jesus

"Love has no meaning if it isn't shared. Love has to be put into action. Intense love does not measure it just gives." ~Mother Teresa

Oh, Father God, thank You for sending Jesus to die on the Cross as the greatest act of Love. Thank You that You are the very essence of love, and You are always showing us Your love for us. Help us to live life-loving others in alignment with Your Word. In Jesus' name, Amen.

JOURNAL/REFLECTIONS

1. According to 1 Corinthians 13, why is love a choice?

_____
_____
_____
_____
_____
_____
_____
_____
_____

2. How is love of the world different from love of the Word?

_____
_____
_____
_____
_____
_____
_____
_____
_____
_____
_____
_____
_____
_____
_____

A Closer Walk With Jesus

3. How would your sphere of influence look different if you were to love by the Word's definition?

Personal Prayer

<u>MORE THAN YOU CAN HANDLE</u>

"But this happened that we might not rely on ourselves but on God, who raises the dead." (2 Corinthians 1:9)

Phone rings and test results came back positive for cancer. Your friend is going through a divorce. A mother just gave birth to a stillborn. A father is visiting his only son, 15, in prison doing life for murder. A teenage girl was drugged and raped. Your husband lost his job. A bride got left at the altar. Parents just lost their son to suicide. You found drugs in your child's room. A single mom does not know how she is going to make ends meet. You have just lost everything you own due to a natural disaster. Your sister just became a widow.

"God won't give you more than you can handle" they said.

Odd, I cannot seem to find that Scripture in the Bible.

We, Christians, have strange ways of comforting those around us in times of suffering. We scramble to find the words to say when someone confesses their life is falling apart. So often, we replace Scripture with traditional wisdom. We say something like, "I am so sorry, but, hey, you know the Bible promises God won't ever give you more in life than you can handle."

There it is—traditional wisdom disguising itself as biblical truth. Do you see what we just did in our attempt to bring comfort? We promised what the Bible does not offer.

The Bible never states God gives us trouble. He does not provide us with tribulation. He does not give us sickness, hardships, or even heartbreak. We need to understand that God is good. Every good and perfect thing comes from Him. (James 1:17) So to say that "God wouldn't give you _____ because it's more than you can handle is not the truth about God's character. We are told that the enemy comes to steal, kill, and destroy, but Jesus came to give life and life more abundantly. (John 10:10) What Scripture does tell us about the hard stuff we walk through is this, "I have said these things to you, that in me you may have peace. In the world, you will have tribulation. But take heart; I have overcome the world." (John 16:33)

Job? Do you think he could handle the grief of seven dead sons and three dead daughters? What about his entire body covered in boils? How about losing all of his wealth in one afternoon? His closest friends mocking him in the middle of his grief. His wife repulsed by him.

How about Joseph? Thrown into a pit by his older brothers who were consumed with jealously. Shortly after, to be sold into slavery, carted off by Egyptians in chains. He works his way up in command while in Egypt to have Potiphar's wife make false accusations against him, causing him to lose his favor and rank, sending him back to jail.

Oh, and then there's Paul. He went to prison numerous times. He is flogged to the point of death. Stoned. He is beaten with rods and shipwrecked three times. Danger from bandits, rivers, his people, wilderness, false brothers, and seas. Labored and toiled, and gone without sleep, food, water, and clothing. Cold and exposed.

Jesus? He was appalled by man. Paraded through the streets, spit on, and mocked. His appearance was so disfigured beyond that of any human being and his form marred beyond human likeness. (Isaiah 54:14) He bore the weight of ALL SINS. Crucified on a cross.

Just like you and me, they, too, were given much more than they could handle. So, the question is then, why? The Apostle Paul wrote: "We do not want you to be uninformed, brothers and sisters, about the troubles we experienced in the province of Asia. We were under great pressure, far beyond our ability to endure, so that we despaired of life itself. Indeed, we felt we had received the sentence of death. But this happened that we might not rely on ourselves but on God, who raises the dead." (2 Corinthians 1:8-9)

Our key verse offers wisdom for us in regard to dealing with more than we can handle. It is so we realize we cannot rely on ourselves, but to rely on God to get us through it. We can consider our present sufferings are not worth comparing with the glory that will be revealed in us. (Romans 8:18) There is so much beauty that can come out of our sufferings. We see the glory that was revealed through the accounts of these men's lives. Job's sufferings resulted in double for his trouble. A double portion was restored to him! Joseph rose to become the prime minister of all Egypt. Saving a nation including the very family that threw him into the pit thirty years prior! (Genesis 41:37-45) Paul went on to write a majority of the New Testament. And then there is Jesus. He defeated death and has given us the opportunity to be reconciled to God the Father because of the blood He shed for us. (Colossians 2:15) We can walk through life this side of eternity in victory over sin and sufferings with resurrection power. Ultimately, spending eternity with God in Heaven.

If God did not give us more than we could handle, there was no need for the death and resurrection of His Son, Jesus Christ. God will allow us to be given more than we can handle, so that we see our need for dependence upon Him. God wants to help us walk through painful things being strengthened in our faith, so that we might be able to encourage others that will walk through something similar we have overcome with His help. (Luke 22:32)

Be blessed by these words from John Newton... on the Christian Life: "Some Christians are called to endure a disproportionate amount of suffering. Such Christians are a spectacle of grace to the Church, like flaming bushes unconsumed, and cause us to ask, like Moses: 'Why is this bush not burned up?' The strength and stability of these believers can be explained only by the miracle of God's sustaining grace. The God who sustains Christians in unceasing pain is the same God -- with the same grace -- who sustains me in my smaller sufferings. We marvel at God's persevering grace and grow in our confidence in Him as He governs our lives." Take heart; if you are suffering affliction and holding fast to a godly response, you are a flaming bush, a spectacle on display!

Father God, thank You that Jesus walked through the ultimate suffering, so that I could be reconciled to You and walk in victory. Help me to be sensitive to those who are suffering around me and have the wisdom to speak into their lives. When I am given more than I can handle, help me to turn to You for comfort and strength in Jesus' name, Amen.

A Closer Walk With Jesus

JOURNAL/REFLECTIONS

1. Have you been told that God will not give you more than you can handle? How did that affect you?

___

2. Why does God allow us to go through more than we can handle?

___

3. Looking at the life of Jesus, how can you have hope to overcome what you are going through?

_____
_____
_____
_____
_____
_____
_____
_____
_____

Personal Prayer

_____
_____
_____
_____
_____
_____
_____
_____
_____
_____
_____
_____
_____
_____

GOD HELPS

"So David and the elders of Israel and the commanders of thousands went to bring up the ark of the covenant of the LORD from the house of Obed-edom with rejoicing. And because God helped the Levites who were carrying the ark of the covenant of the LORD, they sacrificed seven bulls and seven rams." (1 Chronicles 15:25)

Have you ever been in a situation where you needed help? One specific area comes to mind for me, and that was needing God's help with finding my wife. For years, I had strived and pursued girls who ended up being counterfeits, which caused me a lot of confusion. Now, I love reflecting on how I met my wife, Tiffany. It is nothing short of a miracle. For us to have met, it seems 1000 things had to line up exactly right, in order for us to get married. I had to meet an evangelist from Africa and become his driver, driving him throughout the United States. I would have to leave Montana and move to Idaho. A prayer meeting would have to be set up and held at a specific church in Utah, that I would be asked to attend. My wife would have to move from Texas to Utah. She would need to receive an invite to that same church, in order to meet me there.

It is interesting to compare how my relationship with Tiffany took off compared to previous relationships. Remember, I mentioned I had strived with other relationships to make it happen, ultimately ending in heartbreak and confusion. But, with Tiffany, it was different. God helped me discover His will for my life, and that included her. We met, got engaged, and married all in about ten months.

Let us take a closer look at our key verse and discover how God helps us. "And because God helped the Levites who were carrying the ark of the covenant of the Lord." (1 Chronicles 15:25) God will always help us when we are in His will, doing what He has ordained us to do, and doing it the right way. It is a beautiful thing to be in the will of God. Have you ever given thought to the idea of being in the right place at the right time with the right people doing the right thing? What does it take for all of those things to converge? God's help.

God helped the Levites who were carrying the ark. Though the Bible is silent as to what the ark weighed, many have tried to estimate it based on the dimensions given and the materials used. I have seen one estimate as high as 2200 pounds! This would mean each of the 4 men carrying it would be lifting 550 pounds each. It was most likely quite heavy, and this may have been the reason the Israelites, at first, tried to carry it to Jerusalem on a cart pulled by oxen, instead of by 4 men carrying it on 2 poles, as God's Word instructed them. Needless to say, their first try failed miserably when the oxen stumbled, causing Uzzah to put out his hand to the ark of God and take hold of it. As a result, he was struck by the Lord for his error and died there beside the ark. They should have followed God's instructions. Their second attempt went much better, as they obeyed the Lord, and the Bible says that God helped the Levites who were carrying the ark. Isn't that beautiful? He helped them! I believe the Levites who were now carrying the ark did so very carefully; they may have even been afraid considering what happened earlier. But God helped them. Did He give them supernatural strength in that moment to carry it? Did He give them courage and emotional strength after Uzzah's death? I don't know. All I know is He helped them, and He will help you too when you follow His instructions. He will help you perform whatever duty that He calls you to, no matter how difficult it may seem, even if it seems impossible. If you will follow His instruction and trust Him, He will enable you to accomplish the task!

A Closer Walk With Jesus

Just like the Levites, we also need God's help and must look to Him for strength. If we find ourselves tired, exhausted, beaten down, or feeling defeated, we should ask ourselves, "Am I doing the right thing?" If we are doing the right thing and are in His will, but still find ourselves struggling, then we should ask God to come and strengthen us spiritually, physically, and emotionally to accomplish the task. We should ask for wisdom, and He will help. (James 1:5) When God helps us, may we do what the children of Israel did, and offer sacrifice. For us, that may be giving a tithe to the Lord (ten percent of what the Lord has helped us bring in), a love offering (helping someone in need), or maybe it is offering praise to God with our words (sacrifice of praise) and sharing with others how God helped us! It all brings Him glory.

Let us always remember how the Levites got the ark to Jerusalem. God helped them. God will help us, too, when we desire to be closer to Him and when what we are doing will bring Him glory! May we use our gifts and talents for His glory. He will not abandon us in that which He calls us. What He opens, no one can shut, and what He shuts, no one can open. (Revelation 3:7, Isaiah 22:22) When God opens a door for you, walk through that door with joy, and when you get through the door, know that whatever awaits you on the other side, God has equipped you for, and given you what you need. If you follow Him and trust Him with all of your heart, He will help you do what many think is impossible, even as He helped the Levites, so shall He help you. Let Him be your strength and move forward with faith in Him! God bless you all!

Father, help us to learn the lesson of the ark. Help us to do the right thing in the right way, and I trust that when we do that in faith in You, You will help us! May it be said of us, "the Lord helped them," and may You be glorified in our families, and in our lives! I ask all these things of You Father in Jesus' name, Amen.

JOURNAL/REFLECTIONS

1. What was a situation where you needed God's help?

_____
_____
_____
_____
_____
_____
_____
_____
_____
_____

2. What are ways that God helps us?

_____
_____
_____
_____
_____
_____
_____
_____
_____
_____
_____
_____
_____
_____
_____

3. Once we receive God's help, how can we respond like the Levites did?

Personal Prayer

THE LION AND THE BEAR TRAINED DAVID

"And David said to Saul, 'Let no man's heart fail because of him. Your servant will go and fight with this Philistine." "And Saul said to David, 'You are not able to go against this Philistine to fight with him, for you are but a youth, and he has been a man of war from his youth." But David said to Saul, "Your servant used to keep his father's sheep, and when there came a LION, or a BEAR, and took a lamb from the flock, I went after him and struck him and delivered it out of his mouth. And if he arose against me, I caught him by his beard and struck him and killed him. Your servant has struck down both LIONS and BEARS, and this uncircumcised Philistine shall be like one of them, for he has defied the armies of the living God." And David said, "The Lord who delivered me from the paw of the LION and paw of the BEAR will deliver me from the hand of this Philistine." (1 Samuel 17:32)

In history, the Philistine people and the people of Israel were lined up against each other ready for battle; the Philistines on one mountain, and the Israelites on an opposite mountain with a valley between them. The Philistines had a man named Goliath, who was about 9 1/2 feet tall, who was a champion. He uttered a challenge to Israel. Israel was to send a man to fight against him; if Goliath was killed, then the Philistines would become servants to Israel. But if the Israelite warrior was killed, then Israel was to become servants to the Philistines and serve them. The fate of two peoples would come down to a single one on one fight to the death! Could you imagine if we did this today or during World War II? Could you imagine the Nazis sending their best soldier out to the Americans or the Western allies? And the fate of the world coming down to a single fight?

David was ready to fight! He was prepared, trained, and trusted God to lead him into victory. David had been equipped by God to meet this challenge head-on and win! When King Saul tried to discourage him, David responded in confidence by saying, "I have struck down a lion and a bear, and if he arose against me, I grabbed him by his beard and struck him and killed him." That was David's training. That was his bootcamp and he passed the test. To be able to grab a lion or a bear by its beard is hand to hand combat! Those experiences and victories over the wild beasts equipped David for his next fight, Goliath! God had trained David through real life experiences by which David learned of God's protection and faithfulness over his life. He was also anointed with oil by the prophet Samuel and the scripture says, "The Spirit of the Lord came upon David from that day forward." (1 Samuel 16:13) David was now ready. In the ensuing fight, David kills the giant by slinging a stone from his shepherd's sling, striking Goliath in the forehead, bringing him to the ground, where David cuts off his head by using Goliath's own sword.

So, the question stands, what was your lion and bear (your boot camp and training) that prepared you to get where you are today, or where you are going tomorrow? George Washington had his training in the French and Indian War where two horses were shot out from under him. He had four bullet holes shot through his coat, but somehow, they never hit him! It prepared him to lead our country to win our independence. Wikipedia states that Winston Churchill, in World War I, had a close call with death from a piece of shrapnel, which narrowly missed him. It also says when he was younger and working as a journalist in South Africa, that he was captured and became a POW. Miraculously, he escaped from prison and made it to freedom in East Africa. These experiences and others helped shaped him to become the man he was, and I believe prepared him to lead England in its fight against Hitler and the Nazis in World War II. Throughout history, successful men and women were trained and benefited from real-life experiences, which they had received early in life. That training helped them for the future battles they had yet to fight.

May God help all of us to be more like David and to trust God, trust our training, and to be led by Him in our work, families, and lives. It is the diligence, preparation, and work of yesterday, which prepares us for the challenges and opportunities of tomorrow. And when those challenges confront us head-on like Goliath, may we be like David and remember our past experiences of the lion and the bear, and gain strength from them, trusting God to deliver us again and help us gain the victory!

God help us remember where we came from, His faithfulness in times past, the path we took to get here, the good times and bad times, and the skills we learned along the way. Let us give thanks to God for His protection and His blessings. As children of God, we should look to Him to guide us forward, trusting He has equipped us for what lies ahead, and believing that it is God who has armed us with strength for the battle. (Psalms 18:39) Therefore submit to God. Resist the devil and he will flee from you. (James 4:7) Meet the challenge in God's strength and in His name. (1 Samuel 17:45) God bless you. Amen!

JOURNAL/REFLECTIONS

1. Like David, has someone discounted you to accomplish something because of your youth?

_____
_____
_____
_____
_____
_____
_____
_____
_____

2. What was your lion and bear (your boot camp and training) that prepared you to get where you are today, or where you are going tomorrow?

_____
_____
_____
_____
_____
_____
_____
_____
_____
_____
_____

3. In 1 Samuel 17:32, how does David's confidence in the Lord encourage you to face your challenges?

_____
_____
_____
_____
_____
_____
_____
_____
_____

Personal Prayer

_____
_____
_____
_____
_____
_____
_____
_____
_____
_____
_____
_____
_____
_____

<u>VALLEY OF DRY BONES</u>

"The hand of the Lord came upon me and brought me out in the Spirit of the Lord, and set me down in the midst of the valley; and it was full of bones. Then He caused me to pass by them all around, and behold, there were very many in the open valley; and indeed they were very dry. And He said to me, "Son of man, can these bones live?" So I answered, "O Lord God, You know." Again He said to me, "Prophesy to these bones, and say to them, 'O dry bones, hear the word of the Lord! Thus says the Lord God to these bones: "Surely I will cause breath to enter into you, and you shall live. I will put sinews on you and bring flesh upon you, cover you with skin and put breath in you; and you shall live. Then you shall know that I am the Lord."

So I prophesied as I was commanded; and as I prophesied, there was a noise, and suddenly a rattling; and the bones came together, bone to bone. Indeed, as I looked, the sinews and the flesh came upon them, and the skin covered them over; but there was no breath in them. Also He said to me, "Prophesy to the breath, prophesy, son of man, and say to the breath, 'Thus says the Lord God: "Come from the four winds, O breath, and breathe on these slain, that they may live." So I prophesied as He commanded me, and breath came into them, and they lived, and stood upon their feet, an exceedingly great army." (Ezekiel 37:1-10)

The following is life changing. It could change your finances, church, marriage, family, relationships, dreams, and aspirations. Any situation that seems hopeless, broken, or dead can be resurrected to life by the Spirit of God!

More than 2500 years ago, the prophet Ezekiel wrote in Ezekiel chapter 37 verse 1, "The hand of the LORD was upon me, and he brought me out in the Spirit of the LORD and set me down in the middle of the valley; it was full of bones."

A valley is a low area of land between hills or mountains, typically with a river or stream flowing through it. This valley that God showed Ezekiel was not the place of life; rather, it was a valley of death. That which was once alive is now dead! Everywhere Ezekiel looked, he saw death. Even David, in Psalms 23:4, makes mention of "the valley of the shadow of death." Did you know that Death Valley in California is known for the hottest recorded temperature on Earth of 134 degrees? It received its name after thirteen pioneers perished there on a wagon train.

(Verse 2) "And he led me around among them, and behold, there were very many on the surface of the valley, and behold, they were very dry." God leads Ezekiel around the bones to observe that there was no sign of life. These bones had been dead for a while. Decay had consumed the flesh, and the dry bones are all that is left. What in our life, or our surroundings, could these dry bones represent? It could be anything in our life that was once alive and is now dead. Maybe our dreams, ambitions, marriage/relationships, hope, love, passion, ideas, etc.

(Verse 3) "And he said unto me, "Son of man, can these bones live?" And I answered, 'O Lord God, You know.'" Ezekiel was a man of faith. Did you hear his answer? "O Lord God, You know." By answering in such a way, He shows his faith by leaving open the possibility that God can make those bones come alive! May God grant you the same hope and faith to believe that God can resurrect that which now is dead in your life and make it come alive!

(Verse 4) "Then he said to me, 'Prophesy over these bones and say to them, O dry bones, hear the word of the LORD.'" (Verse 5) "Thus says

A Closer Walk With Jesus

the Lord GOD to these bones: Behold, I will cause breath to enter you, and you shall live." God's breath gives life. The Bible says in Genesis 2:7, "Then the LORD God formed the man of dust from the ground and breathed into his nostrils the breath of life, and the man became a living soul." Is there anything or anyone in our life that we need God to breathe on? Let us ask Him now!

(Verse 6) "And I will lay sinews upon you and will cause flesh to come upon you, and cover you with skin, and put breath in you, and you shall live, and you shall know that I am the LORD." God can breathe on your health, marriage, finances, dreams, and visions! Anything around you that is dead, if God breathes on it, it will live! The purpose of this resurrection is so that you will know that He is the Lord!

(Verse 7) "So I prophesied as I was commanded. And as I prophesied, there was a sound, and behold, a rattling, and the bones came together, bone to its bone." Jesus can put the broken pieces of life back together. May we call on Him, ask Him, and believe Him now to resurrect that which has died! Jesus is the resurrection and the life! (John 11:25)

(Verse 8) "And I looked, and behold, there were sinews on them, and flesh had come upon them, and skin had covered them. But there was no breath in them." (Verse 9) "Then he said to me, 'Prophecy to the breath; prophesy, son of man, and say to the breath, 'Thus says the Lord GOD: Come from the four winds, O breath, and breathe on this slain, that they may live.''" God invites Ezekiel to take part in what He is doing! He is to open His mouth and prophesy! The Bible tells us that there is power in our words. (Proverbs 18:21) We must speak life and not death over difficult situations. Instead of telling God how big our problem is, we must tell our problem how big our God is. When we begin to speak out loud God's

Word, God's love, God's power, and God's goodness over our situations, things will begin to shift.

(Verse 10)" So I prophesied as he commanded me, and the breath came into them, and they lived and stood on their feet, an exceedingly great army." Is there anything in your life that has been stolen or lost? Have you lost your sense of joy or your peace? Is your family falling apart? Have you strayed from God's call on your life and do not know how to get back on track? Do you feel hopeless, insignificant, and lacking purpose? Are the puzzle pieces of your life broken and scattered? Do you desire a turnaround, a restoration, and a drawing near to Christ? If so, there is hope. God is able and willing to put back together the broken puzzle pieces of your life, of His calling for you, and make you whole. Run to Jesus right now and call to Him for help. Lay your burdens/sins at His feet and commit yourself to Him. He will not turn you away, but rather receive you with open, loving arms. If God is speaking to you right now concerning a specific situation that He desires to resurrect in your life and you believe He is leading you to speak life over that situation, to prophesy, then prophesy according to verse 4,5,6, and 9. Let the Holy Spirit lead you, believe God, and He shall do it! Jesus is the Resurrection and the Life!

Father, bring life to the dead by the power of the Holy Spirit in Jesus' name! God heal, restore, resurrect, deliver, and renew that which has been lost by Your great power. Breathe on us, our families, our marriages, our work, and our callings, manifesting Your resurrection life, not just to us, but also to the world around us for Your glory. We pray this in Jesus' name, Amen.

A Closer Walk With Jesus

JOURNAL/REFLECTIONS

1. Is there an area in your life that is like the Valley of Dry Bones? Something that was once alive, but is now dead?

_____
_____
_____
_____
_____
_____
_____
_____
_____

2. Do you believe like Ezekiel that God is able to bring your area of "dry bones" back to life?

_____
_____
_____
_____
_____
_____
_____
_____
_____
_____
_____

3. Holy Spirit wants to show you a specific situation that needs a resurrection or a miracle. He is calling you to speak life over that situation, to prophesy, and then prophesy according to verses 4,5,6, and 9.

___

Personal Prayer

___

FINDING GOD

"You will seek Me and find Me when you seek Me with ALL of your heart." (Jeremiah 29:13, emphasis)

Notice the word ALL. The word ALL is the key to make that beautiful promise a reality. I hope all who read that verse will be encouraged. God is not far off. He is not unattainable. Jesus made a way, by His death and resurrection, to reconcile man back to God. A man, by faith in Jesus, can now approach God.

God wants to be pursued. Think relationship. Jesus says in John 17:3, "And this is eternal life, that they KNOW YOU, the only true God, and Jesus Christ whom You have sent." Eternal life is to know the Father, to know Jesus. It's relationship. I know all about famous people and yet do not know them relationally. For example, I know Michael Jordan is a basketball player, 6-time NBA champion, and slam dunk champion, etc., but I do not know Michael Jordan. Likewise, God not only wants mankind to know about Him, but to actually know Him in a real relationship!

Jeremiah 33:3 says, "Call to me, and I will answer you, and will tell you great and HIDDEN THINGS that you have not known." There is a minister from Zambia, David Moses Musonda, whom I have gotten to know quite well over the years. Sometimes, when he randomly looked at the clock and saw the time 3:33, he would call on the Lord. This was a good reminder for him, and God did show Him hidden things, even who the next president would be! This is a practice that I carry on today. If I see

3:33 anywhere, I will call on the Lord. God is all about relationship! Now, we do not have to wait for the time 3:33 to call on the Lord. This verse is an invitation, morning, noon, or night to call on Jesus!

God will show His people HIDDEN THINGS. But they need to call on Him. A man I work with recommended I watch a powerful documentary movie called "Mully,[iv]" which I did. It is a compelling true story of a man who raised, fed, and educated something like 12,000 orphans in Kenya and how they became self-sufficient. After he relocated the children to the country, they needed water. No one had ever found water in that part of Kenya. But God spoke to Him and showed him the exact place to dig a well to find water. Interestingly, they dug until they hit rock. Everyone wanted to quit, except for Mully who believed God. He insisted they keep striking the rock and keep digging. As they obeyed his instruction, they hit the jackpot and the water flowed! (Exodus 17:6) This is similar to when Moses struck the rock and water came out of it. Jesus is the rock. (1 Peter 2:4-8) Life, and that which pertains to life, is only found in Him. The water was hidden, but God showed Mully where the water was hidden! God is the revealer of secret things. Let us remember the words of the prophet Daniel after God revealed to him Nebuchadnezzar's dream and its interpretation. He said of God, "He reveals deep and secret things; He knows what is in the darkness, And light dwells with Him." (Daniel 2:22) Amen!

Proverbs 25:2 says, "It's the glory of God to conceal things, but the glory of kings is to search things out." Myles Munroe once said, "God made Adam and Eve. He made a garden, and He gave them fruit on the trees to eat. But do you know why God never made benches, or tables, or chairs? He hid them in the trees." It was for Adam and Eve and their descendants to discover the uses of trees. What has God placed in or around you to discover?

A Closer Walk With Jesus

In order to begin a relationship with God, one must first be reconciled to God by faith in Jesus Christ to save them. He shed His blood for the forgiveness of sins, dying on the Cross for our sins and by doing so, He made a way to reconcile lost man back to God by the removal of man's sins through His sacrifice on the cross by faith in Jesus Christ. He rose from the dead on the third day and is alive and well, sitting at the right hand of God the Father. It is only by grace, through faith in the Lord Jesus Christ, that mankind is saved and reconciled to God as one of His children. After being saved, in order to grow in that relationship with God, one should read or listen to the Bible as it truly is, as God's Word. We must not read it only as a history book, although it is, but we must read it believing God has something He wants to say to us right now. Read it as a love letter. A letter from our Creator who wants us to know Him. Let us receive His word personally, relationally.

We should also spend time with other believers encouraging one another and praying for one another, for Jesus said in Matthew 18:20, "For where two or three are gathered together in My name, I am there in the midst of them." God is where His people are! That can be church, dinner or wherever two or more believers are gathered together in His name. We must also take time to pray. Being in communion with Father God and taking time to listen to what He wants to say to us. We should take time to stop and reflect on what we have read from His Word, the Bible, our time spent together with other believers, and our time in communion with Him in prayer. Invite the Holy Spirit to speak to your heart, as you reflect on all these things and expect to hear from Him.

Also, pay attention to what happens around you, especially anything out of the ordinary. God spoke to Moses from a burning bush. The bush was burning with fire, but it was not consumed. Moses said, "I will now turn aside and see this great sight, why the bush does not burn." (Exodus 3:3) When he did this, God then spoke to him.

Moses was not to pay attention to all the bushes, or to any other bush that was on fire. He was only to pay attention to the bush that was on fire and yet not consumed. There, he met God. Is it possible for us to miss God in the burning bushes that He sends our way? I think so. We do not want to miss Him. Pay close attention to people, surroundings, coincidences, and things out of the ordinary, and examine those things through the knowledge of the Word of God and through prayer. Always use God's Word. For its use is like that of a compass which will keep us safe from getting lost or confused, so that north will always point north. Haggai 1:5 says, "Now therefore, thus says the Lord of hosts; "Consider your ways!" Ask yourself and God questions concerning your life, in order to discover your calling and purpose here on the Earth and to learn from your mistakes and or successes. Why am I the way I am? Why do I have no money? Why am I rich? Am I a good or a bad friend, husband, wife, or worker? What is the good in my life and what is the bad in my life, and did the decisions I chose contribute to either of them? How has God helped me and where is He leading me? How did I get to where I am today, and connect the dots, whether good or bad? Train your mind to look for God, and your heart to search for Him with all of your heart and you will find Him!

Father, I thank You, that You will be found by those who seek You with all of their hearts! You are good. I thank You that You show Your people hidden things when they call on You! Jesus, you even said the Holy Spirit would tell us things to come (John 16:13) Father, reveal Yourself to us. Show us the hidden things You want us to discover. I ask this all of You Father, in Jesus' name, Amen.

A Closer Walk With Jesus

JOURNAL/REFLECTIONS

1. How does it make you feel to know that God wants to have a personal relationship with you? (John 17:3)

_____
_____
_____
_____
_____
_____
_____
_____
_____
_____

2. What are hidden things that God has shown you because you have sought Him? (Jeremiah 33:3)

_____
_____
_____
_____
_____
_____
_____
_____
_____
_____
_____
_____

3. Why do we find God when we seek Him with all of our heart? (Jeremiah 29:13)

_____
_____
_____
_____
_____
_____
_____
_____

Personal Prayer

_____
_____
_____
_____
_____
_____
_____
_____
_____
_____
_____
_____
_____

BIRTHING PROCESS

"...For as soon as Zion was in labor, she brought forth her children." (Isaiah 66:8)

I believe there is a lot we men can learn through the entire birthing process that can apply to all our lives. Though I have witnessed childbirth three times, I do not pretend to know what my wife, or any other woman, has gone through in the birthing process. All I know is it is nothing short of a miracle.

To begin, let us start with conception. For a baby to be conceived, a lot of things need to line up. You need a man and a woman. You need sperm and an egg. And it needs to be the right time of the month. You get the picture. But once there is the proper alignment of those things, BOOM! A baby is conceived in the womb and nine months later will be born into this world. In life, great projects, callings, and ministries are birthed in a similar fashion. Alignment is needed. First, you will need to have an idea/vision. Next, you need gifts and abilities that match your idea/vision. Last of all, you need courage/strong will to begin. When those three things line up, there is conception in a person's heart (womb) of that which they desire to birth. They have a vision growing inside of them. It might be a vision of a business, career, invention, new home, etc. Once the vision/baby is conceived in the heart, it needs to be protected and nurtured. A woman has to watch what she eats and drinks while pregnant; likewise, you may have to give stuff up, so your dream/vision baby can be nurtured. The first trimester is critical. More babies are miscarried in the first trimester than at any other time of pregnancy. The definition of miscarriage is the expulsion of a baby from the womb before it can survive independently, especially spontaneously, or as the result of an accident. It is essential not to miscarry, or to give birth to something too early. Think of an 18-year-old or anyone receiving a large inheritance before they are mature enough to handle it. It could destroy them if they are not prepared and ready for it. It could be wasted! Just as a baby needs to go full term, so it is with whatever you have conceived in your heart. James 1:4 says, "Allow perseverance (patience) to finish its work so that you may be mature and complete, not lacking anything."

Most abortions also take place in the 1st trimester. John 10:10 says, "The thief comes only to steal and kill and destroy…" If you are not careful, Satan will try to abort your God-given dreams, calling, and destiny.

A sports analogy which might help us better understand is that of Michael Jordan and his desire to play baseball. Michael Jordan was a great basketball player, winning many awards and six championships. In the prime of his career, he briefly retired from basketball to pursue playing baseball, where he played in the Minor League, hoping to move up to the Major League. But after getting no calls from the Major League and baseball then going on strike, he left baseball and returned to basketball where he won three more championships with the Bulls. But what if he would have been simply good enough to play baseball in the Major League, barely making a team. Most likely, he would have been a below average baseball player, rounding out the bottom of the team. If that would have happened and he never returned to basketball, he would have missed out on winning his last three basketball championships with the Bulls and cementing his legacy as one of the greatest to ever play basketball.

Now, I am not saying basketball or baseball was or wasn't God's plan for Jordan's life. That is not the purpose of this analogy and besides, only

God knows. I only share the above story as an analogy for which we can learn from, to be careful to not let earthly distractions or fleshly desires distract us from accomplishing what we are supposed to be doing.

Is it possible for us to miss opportunities to glorify God because of distractions? Yes. Could we be distracted from doing God's will in our lives, in our families, in our churches, and in our communities? I believe so. Instead, I want to be able to say as Paul in 2 Timothy 4:7, "I have fought the good fight, **I have finished the race**, I have kept the faith." I want to say as Jesus said in John 4:34, "My food is to do the will of Him who sent Me, a**nd to finish His work.**" I want said of me what was said of David in Acts 13:36, "For David, after he had **served the purpose of God** in his own generation, fell asleep, . . ." For this to happen, we must be on guard from outside forces that would distract us from our destiny. When distracted, procrastination may set in, and before you know it, you may never get around to birthing your dream, vision, and calling from the Lord. Your time will have passed you by. Distractions aborted your dream. I wonder how often this happens.

I have heard it said that the graveyard is rich. It is rich with dreams that never saw fruition, ideas that were never used, inventions never seen, businesses that were never built, ministries that never got started, and cures which never saw the light of day. Do not take to the grave the ideas, plans, and visions that God has given you today. Step out into the work which He has called you to and bring glory to His name.

In the 2nd trimester, you need to grow in knowledge and refine your skills. You may need to set up appointments with others and receive some training in that which you seek. You will need to get your finances in order. It is time for planning! In the 3rd trimester, many couples get the baby room ready. They set up the crib and purchase diapers and baby clothes. They also come up with a name if they have not already. This is all part of the preparation. It is laying the groundwork!

Last comes labor. Labor can be long or short, but it is not easy. It is work! You will have contractions. You will need to push. This pushing is the process of you taking all that which you have envisioned; your ideas, your plans, and that which was conceived on the inside of you, and pushing all of that out into an outward manifestation of the thing desired. It could mean anxiety, stress, weariness, sleepless nights, long hours, time away from home, or any other challenges you may face. Fear/doubt may set in. But one thing is certain, you have come too far to turn back now. Once labor begins, there is only one option, to push that baby out. To birth what is inside of you, out! It is the outward manifestation of inner thoughts and dreams coming to fruition. John 16:21 says, "Whenever a woman is in labor she has pain, because her hour has come; but when she gives birth to the child, she no longer remembers the anguish because of the joy that a child has been born into the world."

Jesus also endured pain in bringing many sons to glory. (Hebrews 2:10) The Scripture also says of Jesus in Hebrews 12:2: "…who for the joy that was set before Him endured the Cross…" May we do the same, for the joy of the Lord is our strength. (Nehemiah 8:10) Dear reader, the Cross was part of the process of God birthing His sons and daughters. When a woman gives birth to a baby, her water breaks, she bleeds, and she experiences pain. When Jesus died on the Cross, there was blood, there was water, and there was pain. Oh Father God, we praise You for Your plan of salvation brought forth in Jesus Christ, to God be the glory!

In summary, no pain, no gain. Be patient in the pregnancy of your vision/dream. Guard your vision/dream from outside forces, distractions, and doubts. Be disciplined. Remember timing. Do not birth your baby until it is full term. While waiting, add knowledge, prepare, and get your finances in order. When going through suffering, trials, and obstacles, think of the joy that you will have in the end and keep laboring!

Father God, my prayer is not to birth just anything, but to birth that which You have placed inside of us. To birth our God-given calling and destiny, which is from You! That the gifts and talents You have blessed us with would be used for Your glory. You are Creator and it is only in You that we find meaning. Let us look within ourselves and let us see what You see and discover what You have placed there. Holy Spirit blow on those places of our hearts and bring to life inside us Your call, vision, and purpose that You created for us. Protect it from miscarriage and abortion. I ask all these things of You Father, in Jesus' name, Amen.

JOURNAL/REFLECTIONS

1. What visions or dreams has God given you that are in the process of being birthed?

_____
_____
_____
_____
_____
_____
_____
_____
_____

2. Why is it important to let patience have its perfect work in the birthing process of your vision or dream? (James 1:4)

_____
_____
_____
_____
_____
_____
_____
_____
_____
_____
_____

3. Why is it necessary to guard your vision or dream the Lord has given you? (John 10:10)

_____
_____
_____
_____
_____
_____
_____
_____
_____
_____

Personal Prayer

_____
_____
_____
_____
_____
_____
_____
_____
_____
_____
_____
_____
_____
_____

A PROSPEROUS SOUL

"Beloved, I pray that you may prosper in all things and be in health, just as your soul prospers." (3 John 1:2)

David Hinson, a dear friend of mine, is a great example to me of a man with a prosperous soul. With all the extraordinary things that have taken place in 2020, I remember having a conversation with him and him saying something like, "You know, sometimes I feel like I'm living in a different world than everyone else. Everyone I see seems depressed, scared, anxious, and fearful, which is so foreign to me." He means it, too. He is so full of God's Word and so full of the joy of the Lord that it is visible to see with the naked eye. You can see it in him. The truth and reality of God's Word in his life is greater than what he sees with his natural eyes and hears with his natural ears. He walks by faith and not by sight. (2 Corinthians 5:7) His life is built on the Rock, Jesus Christ and on His Word. Though the rain descends, the floods come, and the winds blow and beat on his house, it does not fall, because Christ is his foundation. (Matthew 7:24-25) His soul is prosperous, to God be the glory.

Spirit, soul, and body. Man is composed of all three. It is interesting to note that man is made in God's image and from the Bible, we know that God is: God the Father, God the Son, and God the Holy Spirit. 3 in 1. Somewhere, I heard someone put it this way, "Man is a spirit. Man has a soul. Man lives in a body." The soul is a person's mind, will, and emotions. The fact that we have a spirit, soul, and body is found in 1 Thessalonians 5:23, which says, "And the very God of peace sanctify you wholly, and I pray God your whole spirit and soul and body be preserved blameless unto the coming of our Lord Jesus Christ." Hebrews 4:12 says, "For the word of God is quick, and powerful, and sharper than any two-edged sword, piercing even to the dividing asunder of soul and spirit…" (soul and spirit are different). In our opening verse, the apostle John brings attention to the soul. In 3 John 1:2, John writes to a man named Gaius, "I pray that you may prosper in all things and be in health, just as your soul prospers." (KJV reads "even as your souls prospers.")

What is the key to prospering and being in good health? A prosperous soul! A prosperous mind, will, and emotions. Your soul receives its nutrients from what you feed it and what you feed your soul, will affect what you believe. What you believe will have an effect on the entire outcome of your life, whether for good or for bad.

If you only feed your soul worldly music, Hollywood movies, news media, pornography, worldly attractions, etc. and nothing good, then your soul will be sick, dark, depressed, confused, fearful, anorexic, and on life support. But if your soul is feeding on God's Word, God's truth, God's faithfulness, and life, then your soul will be healthy, full of life, full of hope, and have love, joy, and peace. It all depends on what you are feeding on. If you feed on garbage, your life will manifest sin/garbage, which leads to death. (Romans 6:23) But if you feed on Christ, you will manifest life, which is only found in Him! Let us never forget that Jesus is the Bread of Life! (John 6:35) Let us feed on Him!

When a person is void of hope and does not see themselves as valuable or of any importance, their soul has been poisoned and made sick by lies. That is what happens when a person is contemplating suicide. Satan is lying to them saying, "There is no hope for you, year after year you will still be feeling the same pain, hurt, and disappointment. You might as well end it now and free yourself." If that is you, God wants to destroy that lie with the truth of His Word, letting you know you are valuable to Him. So valuable, He sent His Son Jesus to die on the Cross for your sins to save you! John 3:16 says, "**For God so loved the world** that He gave His only begotten Son, that whoever believes in Him should not perish but have everlasting life." Believe on Jesus, call on His name, and He will save You! (Romans 10:13)

We must be careful what we are eating. A woman can look at the models on magazine covers and feel fat, ugly, and unattractive. Why is that? Because she is believing Satan's lies and comparing herself to what he tells her she should look like. Oh that wicked deceiver who molests the souls of man, tormenting them and blinding them from the truth of Jesus Christ who is willing to set them free! Do not listen to Satan or argue with him or else you will find yourself depressed, feeling hopeless, confused, and worthless. He is a liar and the father of it. (John 8:44) His plan is to steal, kill, and destroy. (John 10:10) If we have believed the lies of the enemy, the question then is, how does one get free?

The truth will set you free. Jesus is Truth. (John 14:6) God's Word is Truth. (John 17:17) Jesus says in John 8:32, "And ye shall know the truth, and the truth shall make you free." John 17:17 says, "Sanctify them in the truth; your word is truth." In John 14:6, Jesus said to him, "I am the way, the truth, and the life. No one comes to the Father except through Me." Truth is the antidote to the poisonous lies of Satan and the world.

Paul says, "And do not be conformed to this world, but be transformed by the renewing of your mind, that you may prove what is that good and acceptable and perfect will of God." (Romans 12:2) We must run to God's Word, and devour it. The Bible is our textbook. The Holy Spirit is the teacher. (John 14:26) He is also known as the Spirit of Truth. (John 16:13)

If we receive His Word as truth and yield to the Holy Spirit's teaching, then God will correct our wrong thinking, renewing our minds, and rewiring our brains, which will set us free from living under the darkness and tyranny of lies. God's Word acts as a spiritual cleaning agent. Jesus said to His apostles, "Now ye are clean through the word which I have spoken unto you." (John 15:3) Receive God's Word and be free and be clean, and your soul will prosper.

If you desire to have a prosperous soul, then you must feed on God's Word and put to practice what Paul says in Philippians 4:8-9, "Finally, brethren, whatever things are true, whatever things are noble, whatever things are just, whatever things are pure, whatever things are lovely, whatever things are of good report, if there is any virtue and if there is anything praise worthy—meditate on these things. The things which you learned and received and heard and saw in me, these do, and the God of peace will be with you." These instructions, if put to practice in our lives, will aid in the prosperity of our souls.

The truly prosperous soul is a soul which is full of the Word of God, whose mind thinks God's thoughts from the Word in everyday life situations, analyzing everything with the truth of God's Word and acting accordingly to that which is written therein. A prosperous soul is a soul whose will is in line with God's will. A prosperous soul is one whose emotions are moved by the truth of God's Word, such as to rejoice with those who rejoice and weep with those who weep. (Romans 12:15) It will bear one another's burdens. (Galatians 6:2) It will love its neighbor as itself. (Mark 12:31) It will love its enemies and bless those who curse them. It will do good to those who hate them and pray for those who spitefully use them and persecute them. (Matthew 5:44) Its love will be the kind found in 1 Corinthians 13. It bears all things, believes all things, hopes all things, and endures all things. (1 Corinthians 13:7) That is a prosperous soul. A soul whose mind, will, and emotions are in line with God's Word, feeding on it for its nutrition. It is a soul which reacts to God's Word and not to the circumstances around them. That person will prosper in business, family, health, and their relationship with God and mankind. Did you know that our physical health is connected to our souls? Even research has shown that poor health of the human body can be related to anxiety, stress, and fear, which proceed out of the soul.

A prosperous soul is vital in every aspect of our lives. To have a prosperous soul, we need to believe the truth of God's Word over the lies of the devil. Jesus said in Matthew 4:4, "Man shall not live by bread alone, but by every word that comes from the mouth of God."

Father, help all who read this to prosper in their souls! May Your Word cleanse us from all lies and false beliefs that are weighing us down and keeping us from fulfilling Your will in our lives. Give us the grace to meditate on Your Word! For Your Truth truly sets men free! I ask all these things of You Father, in Jesus' name, Amen.

JOURNAL/REFLECTIONS

1. What is the key to prospering and being in good health? (3 John 1:2)

2. When we have bought the lies of Satan and our soul is sick, how do we get free so that our soul can prosper? (John 8:32, John 17:17)

3. Why is a prosperous soul vital in every aspect of life?

Personal Prayer

TRAVIS'S TESTIMONY

"Turn to me and be saved all the ends of the earth! For I am God, and there is no other." (Isaiah 45:22)

As an adolescent growing up in Montana on the banks of the Yellowstone River, God would visit me in the evening times. I remember lying on my bed looking out my window, seeing the moon, and listening to the wind blowing through the trees, and it was there that God would speak to my heart. What were our talks like? He spoke to me about the call placed on my life and showed me He had called me to be His messenger. God would reveal to me His might, His power, and His Majesty through His Creation day after day, night after night. He would invite me to follow Him. Instead of accepting His invitation, I chose to chase after girls and my selfish ways of turning God down night after night. There were times I can remember having this strong impression that God was calling me to speak for Him, like a messenger, but I was not ready for that, and I wanted to do my own thing. I often wondered what others would think of me if I decided to follow Jesus. And God would say to me, "Why do you care what others would think? Why are you scared? Look at the stars, the moon, and look at the river. I have created all these; I have created all things!" I would get the sense of God's majesty, power, and largeness in those moments, but still, I was not ready. But He was faithful and kept pursuing me!

I will never forget the day when, as a junior in high school, my entire life changed. Earlier, my girlfriend and I had broken up. But then one day, sometime after, I found out from a friend in school that she had moved on and was dating another guy. I was not ready for that news. Insecurity crept in and I felt miserable and was crushed by the news. As I lost control that night in my room, I cried like a baby, and in my distress, instead of running from God, I ran to God. In my brokenness, I cried out to Him saying something like, "Jesus help me, Jesus help me, Oh God help!" I did not know what else to do but to cry out to God. I needed comfort, I need help, and I needed Him.

Did you know the Bible says, "For everyone who calls on the name of the Lord will be saved." (Romans 10:13) It is true. He not only answered my cry for help, but He also saved me! That night changed the rest of my life. I have never been the same since. After that night, I became hungry for God's Word. I brought my Bible to school and when I got some free time, I would open it up and read. When I got home from school, I would shut myself up in my room and read the Bible some more; like the prophet Jeremiah, I devoured His Word. (Jeremiah 15:16) God was moving in my life. He quickly restored my relationship with my mom and also started blessing my relationship with my dad. As my relationship with God grew, and He continued to transform me, my parents could see the change in me, and even canceled my curfew. The rules and laws that I previously had to follow from my parents were no longer needed, because I was no longer bound by sin. I was free. I was now under the law of love, and where there is love, there is no need for law. (Matthew 22:37-40)

But what is amazing about this all is I was not alone in this transformation process. God was moving in my high school, and some of my friends got saved around this time, as well. The work God did in our high school, at this time, was incredible. In my senior year, not one player missed a football game because of an injury. One time, our tailback got hurt in the game, and we prayed for him right there in the huddle. God healed him. On the bus ride home, he got up and gave glory to God in front of the whole team! Another time, I can remember getting prayer at halftime from a classmate for an injury I had received, and I was able to play the rest of the game. My senior year was so different than the other years of me playing football. The atmosphere changed my senior year. We prayed together and for one another, and also won our conference. It was an awesome experience that has marked me for life. God was at work in our lives, and it was evident. We brought our Bibles to school and even got to have some spiritual talks with our teachers about God and the Bible. We would pray for people right there in the school halls in front of lockers! People were open and receptive because God was moving. We would often meet in the mornings for prayer before school, and sometimes in the evening, we would have Bible study or one of my friends would lead us in worship on His guitar. High school was one of the most significant seasons in my life. God not only saved me, but in His graciousness, surrounded me with other believers that were hungry for Him and His Word, as well.

In closing, let us remember these powerful words from God.

"Turn to me and be saved all the ends of the earth! For I am God, and there is no other." (Isaiah 45:22)

Father, may this invitation from You burn in the hearts of all who read it, and whoever has not responded to this invitation, I pray they will now. I ask this in Jesus' name, Amen.

JOURNAL/REFLECTIONS

1. Has God used something devastating you went through to bring you back to Himself?

_____
_____
_____
_____
_____
_____
_____
_____
_____
_____

2. Have you experienced a time of brokenness or distress and cried out to the Lord and seen Him answer? How did that change your situation? (Romans 10:13)

_____
_____
_____
_____
_____
_____
_____
_____
_____
_____
_____
_____

3. How can having an encounter with the Living God change those around you?

Personal Prayer

GOD OF THE IMPOSSIBLE

"But Jesus looked at them and said, 'With man, this is impossible, but with God all things are possible.'" (Matthew 19:26)

Have you ever faced something in life that just seemed impossible? That thing that caused you to cry out to God to make it possible. Maybe, it was needing to pass an exam, a wayward son or daughter, or a financial miracle? Are you in need right now of a miracle from God? A miracle in your body? Or in your family? If so, be encouraged. God can do it! Ask Him and believe! God performs the miraculous. (Luke 1:37) God is in the business of rescuing. (Psalm 107:19)

Our key verse in Matthew 19:26 declares, "But with God all things are possible." This is evident in the Christmas story. Let us review the supernatural workings of God found therein. Jesus' birth was supernatural and a miracle. He was born of a virgin! (Isaiah 7:14) The star, which led the wise men, was supernatural. (Matthew 2:9-10) The angelic visitations to Mary, Joseph, and the shepherds, and the dreams given by God to Joseph and the wisemen warning them about Herod, were all supernatural. (Matthew chapters 1 and 2; Luke chapters 1 and 2)

With God, all things are possible. Think about the star, and how it went before the wisemen and stood over where the young child was laying. The star reminds us of how God can lead us, and His precision is exact. Jesus is called "The Good Shepherd." Follow Him and let Him lead you. Let us not forget the shepherds who were visited by an angel who told them they would find the baby wrapped in swaddling cloths and lying in a manger. Then, many angels appeared praising God, which the shepherds saw. And yes, God still sends angels today. Let us remember this verse, Hebrews 11:14: "Are they not all ministering spirits sent out to serve for the sake of those who are to inherit salvation?" The ministry of angels is to serve/minister to those who are to be saved!

What about dreams? Joseph resolved to divorce Mary over the pregnancy, but as he considered these things, an angel of the Lord appeared to him in a dream, saying, "… Joseph, son of David, do not fear to take Mary as your wife, for that which is conceived in her is from the Holy Spirit. She will bear a son, and you shall call His name Jesus, for He will save His people from their sins." (Matthew 1:20-21) Matthew 2:12 tells how the wisemen were warned in a dream not to return to Herod. Matthew 2:13 tells how Joseph was told by an angel in a dream, "Rise, take the child and his mother, and flee to Egypt, and remain there until I tell you, for Herod is about to search for the child, to destroy him." Then, after Herod died, an angel of the Lord appeared in a dream to Joseph in Egypt, saying, "Rise, take the child and his mother and go to the land of Israel, for those who sought the child's life are dead." (Matthew 2:19-20) The dreams speak of God's warnings and communications to men. God still warns and communicates to men through dreams today. I have experienced some God dreams in my own life and look forward to having more of them. Spending time in prayer and in study of the Bible will help you in understanding the dreams that you dream and always ask God to give you the interpretation.

Let us be encouraged that we serve a powerful God who can do anything. God is the God of the supernatural and the Christmas story is full of the supernatural. The birth of Jesus reminds us that nothing is impossible for God and reminds us of God's plan of salvation. Jesus, the Saviour of the world, born as a baby, to later die on the cross for our sins, that whoever believes in Him should not perish but have everlasting life. (John 3:16) Faith in Jesus saves believers from their sins and from hell, and reconciles them to God the Father as one of His children. Salvation is the ultimate act of God. God bless you and know that God is the author of salvation, miracles, wisdom, and all that you need.

Father, thank You for Jesus! Thank You for Your plan of salvation through Jesus! Thank You for the sacrifice of Your Son to save mankind! I thank You that for whoever calls on the name of the LORD shall be saved. (Romans 10:13) Lead us like You led the wisemen. Speak to us like You spoke to Mary and Joseph. Give us dreams of instruction and warning and help us to follow You wherever You may lead. Have Your way in our lives. I pray this in Jesus' name, Amen!

JOURNAL/REFLECTIONS

1. Have you ever faced something in life that just seemed impossible?
___

2. From angelic visitations, the star of David, and dreams, God was always speaking and guiding. In your life, what has God used to show you He is speaking to you and guiding you?
___

3. How does Jesus' birth and God's plan of salvation reveal to you that God can do the impossible in your life?

Personal Prayer

OUT OF EGYPT

"When Israel was a child, then I loved him and called my son out of Egypt." (Hosea 11:1)

Bondage is the state of being bound by or subjected to some external power or control. I am curious if I am the only one that has been in bondage to something? Drugs, alcohol, pornography, lying, gluttony, fear, jealousy, bitterness, or greed? Maybe, in contrast, you are one also like me who has experienced great deliverance and promise from the very thing that had you enslaved?

So, let us take a more in-depth look into some questions around our key verse. In Scripture, Egypt is a representation of the best that man has to offer. It represents the world, the flesh, the natural man, and our sin. (Ephesians 2:8-9) But man's best will never meet or be accepted by God's standard. It falls short. How does one get out of Egypt? God sends a deliverer! In the Old Testament, the deliverer was named Moses. God used him to bring the Israelites out of bondage from the Egyptians. Moses was a prophetic picture of Jesus who would come in the New Testament.

Moses prophesied about Jesus saying in Deuteronomy 18:15, "The Lord your God will raise up for you a prophet like me from among you, from your brothers—it is to him you shall listen." In Verse 18:18, God says to Moses, "I will raise up for them a prophet like you from among their brothers. And I will put my words in his mouth, and he shall speak to them all that I command him." Then, God says in Verse 19, "And it shall come to pass, that whosoever will not hearken unto my words which he shall speak in my name, I will require it of him." Peter says in Acts 3:23 concerning that prophet, "And it shall come to pass that every soul, which will not hear that prophet shall be destroyed from among the people." That prophet is Jesus! Jesus says in John 14:6, "I am the way, and the truth, and the life. No one comes to the Father except through me."

All roads do not lead to God and eternal life. There is only one way, and that is through Jesus! For anyone to come out of Egypt, the place their sin has them in bondage, they must place their faith in Jesus for salvation. He will not let them down. Jesus is the great Redeemer. His blood has paid sin's debt. The ransom has been paid with His blood! Come out of Egypt and into the Promised Land and take to heart Paul's words in Galatians 5:1 which say, "Stand fast therefore in the liberty by which Christ has made us free, and do not be entangled again with a yoke of bondage." God bless you all.

Father, I pray for those reading this who want out of Egypt, I ask that You would extend grace to the reader and impart faith into their hearts to believe on You Jesus and be saved! You are the great deliverer. Deliver the soul that comes to you out of depression, out of fear, out of addiction, and out of darkness, into Your marvelous light. (1 Peter 2:9) I ask this all of You Father, in Jesus' name, Amen.

A Closer Walk With Jesus

JOURNAL/REFLECTIONS

1. Do you have any bondage in your life that you need freedom from right now? If not, have you experienced freedom from bondage that you were in?

_____
_____
_____
_____
_____
_____
_____
_____
_____

2. How does it feel knowing that Jesus' blood covers you and enables you to be a slave to sin no longer? (Galatians 5:1)

_____
_____
_____
_____
_____
_____
_____
_____
_____
_____

3. If you are wanting out of Egypt (your bondage), what is stopping you?

Personal Prayer

MAN, OF A DIFFERENT SPIRIT

"And now, behold, the Lord has kept me alive, just as he said, these forty-five years since the time that the Lord spoke this word to Moses, while Israel walked in the wilderness. And now, behold, I am this day eighty-five years old. I am still as strong today as I was in the day that Moses sent me; my strength now is as my strength was then, for war and for going and coming. So now give me this hill country (mountain) of which the Lord spoke on that day, for you heard on that day how the Anakim (Giants) were there, with great fortified cities. It may be that the Lord will be with me, and I shall drive them out just as the LORD said." (Joshua 14:10-12)

I love history and am fascinated by those individuals who stood apart from the crowd in achieving impossible tasks and in changing the world. For example, where did Columbus get his strength of resolve to sail west when some thought he would sail off the edge of the world? There is a story written about his first journey where some of his crew planned to do evil to him, even "planned to throw into the sea" (d'-Anghera 1:59-60). Where did his great perseverance come from? Have you ever considered the inner conviction and belief that he carried inside of himself? What made the Wright brothers (inventors of the first successful airplane) believe that flight was possible when it had never been done before? Where did Martin Luther find the strength to go against the flow and the norms of his day? These individuals stood apart from the crowd and had deep inner convictions. Likewise, so did Caleb who we read about in our opening verse. I get the feeling this 85-year-old man ran circles around men half his age. He knew that if the LORD was with him, he would drive the giants off the mountain. He still had strength in his body for war, even when he was

85. He was different than the others. He had courage. He had what the Bible says, "a different spirit in him," and he followed the Lord fully (Numbers 14:24). Caleb was a special man.

In our key verse, it has been forty-five years since Caleb first spied out the Promised Land. He is as strong now at eighty-five as he was when he was forty. Caleb, at age eighty-five, drives out the giants, conquers the mountain, and possesses his inheritance! What amazing patience and faith he exhibited. Hundreds of thousands, possibly millions, of people died from the previous generation, because they did not believe God that they could defeat the giants and the nations, which inhabited the land. Everyone twenty years and older died from that 1st generation. That was their judgement for unbelief. Forty-five years later, only Joshua and Caleb remained alive from that generation, and only those two men from that generation would enter the Promised Land.

Is it possible to be pregnant with God's Word? God's Word is seed. (Luke 8:11) When it is heard and believed, it takes root in the heart of the believer and grows into the fruition of its divine purpose, producing what God intended it for. (Isaiah 55:11) What did Mary tell the angel Gabriel when he told her that she would have a son? She said, "Behold, I am the servant of the Lord; let it be to me according to your word." Mary believed the Word of God unto her and it was so! Caleb also believed the Word of God and was blessed as a result. God told the people in Exodus 23:20-33 that if they obeyed the Lord, then God would bring them into the land and He would cut off the nations, which were there and deliver the inhabitants of the land into their hand. The first time they reached the Promised Land, Caleb said to the people, "Let us go up at once and take possession, for we are well able to overcome it." (Numbers 13:30) He believed God's Word. Caleb, along with Joshua, even said that the inhabitants of the land were their bread! (Numbers 14:9) Amazing faith! God said the following about Caleb in Numbers 14:24, "But my servant Caleb, because he has a different spirit and has followed me fully, I will bring into the land into which he went, and his descendants shall possess it." In Numbers 14:30, God says, "Not one shall come into the land where I swore that I would make you dwell, except Caleb the son of Jephunneh and Joshua the son of Nun."

Caleb entered the land. He succeeded in battle. Joshua 15:14 says, "And Caleb drove out from there, the three sons of Anak, Sheshai and Ahiman and Talmai, the descendants of Anak." Behold the blessing of God which resides on them who trust Him.

Beloved, let us seek God concerning our Promised Land. May the Lord help us find it, discover it, and possess it. What is God's Word concerning you, your family, your work, and your destiny? Ask God. Jesus says in Mathew 7:7-8, "Ask, and it will be given to you; seek, and you will find; knock, and it will be opened unto you. For everyone who asks receives, and the one who seeks finds, and to the one who knocks it will be opened." And once HE has spoken to you, it is money in the bank. To withdraw and enjoy the blessing, you only need to believe and keep on believing, and you shall receive!

2 Corinthians 5:7 says, "For we walk by faith not by sight."

Sometimes, in the natural, everything may seem like it is falling apart, or that time has passed us by. Do not believe it. Keep trusting God and you shall be blessed like Caleb. Walk by faith and not by sight. Walk by faith and not your age, or your feelings, or what others say. Walk by faith in what God says and you shall be blessed.

Isaiah 40:31 says, "But they who wait for the Lord shall renew their strength; they shall mount up with wings like eagles; they shall run and not be weary; they shall walk and not faint."

Daniel 11:32 says, "... but the people who know their God shall stand firm and take action."

I believe there are blessings awaiting each one of us, both in work, family, and personal lives. May God help us to discover our mission, our destiny, and then to embrace it, possess it, and walk in it, to its fullness. The more we walk in what He has called us, the more our work will be blessed, our family will be blessed, and our lives will be blessed.

Father, help us to inherit everything that You have allotted to us. Help us each reach our full potential, both corporately and individually! Feed our hearts, our spirits, with Your Word, and with Your promises. Impregnate us with Your Word, Your vision, and give us the strength and grace to walk what You have spoken and to possess our Promised Land, our destiny! Be glorified in us. Bless us and draw us each closer to Your heart! I ask all of this of You Father, in Jesus' name, Amen.

JOURNAL/REFLECTIONS

1. Have you done something in life that was quite remarkable at an age that most would not have accomplished?

_____
_____
_____
_____
_____
_____
_____
_____
_____
_____

2. What is God's Word concerning you, your family, your work, and your destiny?

_____
_____
_____
_____
_____
_____
_____
_____
_____
_____
_____
_____
_____

3. Why is it important to walk by faith and not by sight? (2 Corinthians 5:7)

Personal Prayer

JIM'S TESTIMONY

"So then faith comes by hearing and hearing by the word of God." (Romans 10:17)

I want to share with you about a man I have come to love. A man I worked for about thirteen months before God gave me the job I am at now. Let us call his name *Jim*. Jim is a businessman home builder/carpenter. Jim loves the Lord and has entire sections of the Bible memorized. He loves to minister God's Word.

Every Tuesday morning, he has prayer at his house with a group of men, before they go to work. He has a Wednesday morning gathering he leads every week at a local coffee shop. Jim also leads and shares God's Word with another men's group, made up of many different churches, that meets every Friday morning for breakfast at a local restaurant in town. Sometimes, Jim preaches to the entire restaurant, and they do not mind, because he has been doing this for years. Jim does all of this while running his business and serving as an elder at his church.

Jim is married with two sons. The oldest is in the military, while the other son has been in and out of jail since I have known him. Let us call that son *Mike*. Mike became caught up with the wrong crowd and got into drugs. Jim's faith, though, has never wavered. He knows his son will one day serve the Lord for that is what God told him.

Jim raised his boys the right way, bringing them to work with him and teaching them the benefits of hard work. His boys grew up in church and know the Bible. Through the years, Jim has received some prophecies concerning his sons, that they would be men who would serve the Lord and be used by God. Right now, he does not see the fulfillment of that prophecy with Mike. But Jim does not doubt it. He trusts God with all his heart that God will get ahold of his son and that his son will serve the Lord, and God will fulfill His Word spoken over him.

Although I have not asked Jim directly, I know he believes the following verse over his household. Acts 16:31 says, "So they said, 'Believe on the Lord Jesus Christ, and you will be saved, you and your household.'"

And the next verse, I think I have heard him share, so I know he believes it. 1 Timothy 1:18 says, "Timothy, my son, I am giving you this instruction in keeping with the prophecies previously made about you, so that by recalling them you may fight the good fight."

Jim told me once, "All you need is a word from God, and you can stand on that promise." How true! Jim believes that and lives that out in his life. Even when Mike got in a horrible motorcycle accident, which should have killed him, Jim stood on God's Word concerning his son, that one day his son will serve the Lord. Miraculously, God spared his son's life in that wreck. Jim did not let fear creep into his life. He trusted God then, and he is still trusting God today.

That, essentially, was what Paul was telling Timothy in the above verse. That by recalling the prophecies that were given to Timothy, Timothy would fight the good fight. You can take to the bank what God says! Knowing and believing what God says will keep you in the fight, even though everything around you may seem contrary to what He spoke. Think of Noah. He built an ark to save his household because He believed God's Word. The flood was coming. No matter what anyone else said or how ridiculous it may have looked to his neighbors, Noah knew the flood was coming. Hearing, believing, and acting upon the Word of God is what saved Noah's family. Hearing God and believing what He says will keep you in the fight and save you and others from destruction. Without God's Word, many would give up.

Our key verse Romans 10:17 states: "So then faith comes by hearing, and hearing by the word of God." We all need to hear God's Word. We need to see what God is showing us about our lives, about our finances, and about our hearts, and where He wants to take us and to do with us. When God speaks to us about anything, whether through the Bible or through prayer, believe it! Remember what Mary, Jesus' mother, said to the servants concerning Jesus? She said in John 2:5, "Whatever he says to you, do it." (The most significant advice ever!)

Beloved, what is Jesus saying to you right now? Remember, we must pay attention to our conscience; it is one of the ways in which He speaks to us. Listen to your pastor and the men and women of God in your life. Listen to God's Word the Bible. And friends, when you hear Him speak, believe what He says and act accordingly. If we believe and act on what He says, it will change our circumstances. Sometimes, what He says may seem the exact opposite of our circumstances, and that is okay. We must make a choice to believe it and watch Him make the impossible possible, turning around our situation. (Matthew 19:26)

Romans 4:17 tells us "… God, who gives life to the dead and calls those things which do not exist as though they did." In Genesis 17, God changes Abram's name to Abraham, which means "Father of many nations." He changed his wife Sarai's name to Sarah, saying, "and she shall be a mother of nations." He did this while Abraham and Sarah had no children from their marriage union. He said this when they were old. They believed God and God performed a miracle in their bodies, and she became pregnant. God can still perform miracles if we believe what He says. Matthew 24:35 says, "Heaven and earth shall pass away, but my words shall not pass away."

Recently, Mike got in a car wreck, and again, the Lord had mercy on him. In the wreck, he broke his foot. Well, one Sunday morning, Mike came to church, which is another miracle. But better yet, during the praise and worship, Mike started to feel things moving in his foot. He felt bones and everything shifting in his foot, being moved. God healed his foot during the worship songs.

Being filled with joy, he went and told his dad Jim. At the end of the service, Jim got up and shared how God healed his son's broken foot to the entire church congregation. He called Mike forward, and Mike walked to the front. He was completely overwhelmed by emotions. He was fist-pumping in praise and, to me, looked like he was crying. God not only healed his foot, but was also at work in his heart. As Paul, the apostle, said in Romans 2:4, "… not knowing that the goodness of God leads you to repentance?"

Mike will one day serve the Lord. God's promises are true. When Jesus died on the Cross, His feet were pierced with a nail. He bled from His feet. The blood shed from His feet is able to redeem any wrong path that any of us have ever taken. Our feet have led us into all sorts of sin, going to the wrong places, doing the wrong things. Our feet led us to those places. We were going the wrong way. Jesus' feet being pierced with the nail and bleeding was done to redeem the wrong paths our feet have taken us down, and to forgive us and cleanse us from our sin that our feet led us into. Mike's feet being healed is a prophetic picture of God's desire to straighten out Mike and get him on the right path, the God path. Jim believes that for Mike and it will come to pass.

I encourage you all, like Mike, to pray for anyone in your life who is going down a destructive path. Pray for God to deliver and redeem their life from sin, wrong choices, and set them on the right path going in the right direction. Pray, hope, and believe! God bless you all!

Father God, thank You for Your redemptive power! I thank You that You are the God of second chances, that You are the God of the repentant. You are merciful and good, and Your love never fails. Set free our loved ones, friends, and family members who are going down the wrong path. Set them free by Your grace and power for Your glory. Draw us all closer to You. I ask these things of You Father, in Jesus' name, Amen.

JOURNAL/REFLECTIONS

1. Why is it important to hear the Word of God? (Romans 10:17)

_____
_____
_____
_____
_____
_____
_____
_____
_____

2. What words from God have you received and are waiting on Him to fulfill? (1 Timothy 1:18)

_____
_____
_____
_____
_____
_____
_____
_____
_____
_____
_____
_____

A Closer Walk With Jesus

3. Remember what Mary, Jesus' mother, said to the servants concerning Jesus? She said in John 2:5, "Whatever He says to you, do it. What is Jesus saying to you right now?

_____
_____
_____
_____
_____
_____
_____
_____
_____

Personal Prayer

_____
_____
_____
_____
_____
_____
_____
_____
_____
_____
_____
_____
_____

POSSESSING YOUR PROMISED LAND

"On that day I swore to them that I would bring them out of the land of Egypt into a land that I had searched out for them, a land flowing with milk and honey, the most glorious of all lands." (Ezekiel 20:6, ESV)

Maybe you are like me and find yourself asking the question, "What exactly is my *promised land*?" Our Promised Land is a land that God has searched out for each one of us. It is precisely for you. He desires to bring you into this land if you will only trust Him. Milk and honey speak of the richness and goodness of this land, the most glorious of all lands!

"So it shall be, when the Lord your God brings you into the land of which He swore to your fathers, to Abraham, Isaac, and Jacob, to give you large and beautiful cities which you did not build, houses full of all good things, which you did not fill, hewn-out wells which you did not dig, vineyards and olive trees which you did not plant-when you have eaten and are full." (Deuteronomy 6:10-11)

Our Promised Land is a place full of God's grace, getting what we do not deserve! It is not man's work. We will not get there by our effort. This point is emphasized when the verse says: to give you large and beautiful cities which you did not build, houses full of all good things, which you did not fill, hewn-out wells which you did not dig, and vineyards and olive trees which you did not plant. This Scripture paints a beautiful picture of the grace of God given to us. Oh, that we would trust Him.

Deuteronomy 11:10-12 says, "For the land that you are entering to take possession of it is not like the land of Egypt, from which you have come, where you sowed your seed and irrigated it, like a garden of vegetables. But the land that you are going over to possess is a land of hills and valleys, which drinks water by the rain from heaven, a land that the LORD your God cares for. The eyes of the LORD your God are always upon it, from the beginning of the year to the end of the year."

This verse compares Egypt (the natural order of doing things) to the Promised Land (where God is the one doing things). In Egypt, you plant the seed and irrigate to get your harvest. In the Promised Land, God cares for the land. It is a land of hills and valleys, which drinks water by the rain from Heaven (God irrigates, not man), a land that the Lord your God cares for. The Promised Land is a place of faith. If God does not send the rain, you starve and die. Egypt is a picture of the best man can do, and the Promised Land is a picture of what God can do. It is a grace-filled land that takes faith to inherit. I do not know about you, but I want to inherit and possess my Promise Land.

Numbers 13:23 says, "And they came to the valley of Eshcol and cut down from there a branch with a single cluster of grapes, and they carried it on a pole between two of them; they also brought some pomegranates and figs."

In this land of grace, which is only attained by faith, a single cluster of grapes was carried on a pole between two men. What a blessing. I sure would have loved to taste those grapes! There is blessing for you, too, in your Promised Land. Psalms 34:8 says, "Oh, taste and see that the LORD is good; Blessed is the man who trusts in him!"

A Closer Walk With Jesus

Our lives will not reach their full potential if we do not inherit our Promise Land. We were made for our Promised Land, and our Promised Land was made for us. We must not settle for mundane. We would be wise not to choose the path of least resistance and become a slave to our circumstances. An all-powerful God created us; we must trust Him to help us possess our Promised Land.

The Promised Land in the above verses was a literal land in the Old Testament, but symbolized Heaven/eternal life/salvation in Jesus Christ in the New Testament. There is the here and now Promised Land, and the hereafter Promised Land. Let us look at some examples of this through the lives of Mary, John the Baptist, and Esther. Mary's here and now Promised Land was to birth Jesus Christ as a virgin. Her womb was to carry the Creator of the world. John the Baptist's here and now Promised Land was that of a forerunner, to prepare a people for the Lord Jesus through a baptism of repentance. Queen Esther's here and now Promised Land was to become queen and risk her own life by coming before the King uninvited to ask for the salvation of her people from Haman's evil plot. These were their destinies!

Now the question is, what is your God-given destiny? What is your Promised Land? What were you placed on this Earth to accomplish? Ask God, talk to Him about it! Discover it and possess it with God's help.

Father God, I bless Your name. I praise You for Your grace and goodness! Show each of us what we were created for and why we were put on this Earth. You know God. By Your grace, help us to walk by faith in You and accomplish all that You want us to achieve. Give us favor, and strengthen us in our work for Your glory! I ask all these things of You Father, in Jesus' name, Amen.

JOURNAL/REFLECTIONS

1. Compare the difference between Egypt and the Promise Land.

2. What is your Promise Land, your God-given destiny?

3. Your Promise Land is full of grace. According to Deuteronomy 6:10-11, how does it make you feel knowing God is going to give you something you do not deserve?

_____
_____
_____
_____
_____
_____
_____
_____
_____

Personal Prayer

_____
_____
_____
_____
_____
_____
_____
_____
_____
_____
_____
_____
_____

SLAYING THE GIANTS

". . . The land through which we have gone as spies is a land that devours its inhabitants, and all the people whom we saw in it are men of great stature. There we saw the giants (the descendants of Anak came from the giants), and we were like grasshoppers in our own sight, and so we were in their sight." (Numbers 13:32-33)

One of Satan's tactics in preventing you from possessing your Promise Land is to fill your Promised Land with giants. The giants of fear, poverty, lies, perversions, distractions, unforgiveness, unbelief, and the list goes on. These giants are real. They are demonic, satanic, and they live and survive in a climate of our own making. If we are not careful, they will steal our future, our destiny, and our inheritance. We must destroy them, we all must, to inherit our Promised Land.

The giants of the original Promised Land descended from the "sons of God (angels) who sinned" by sleeping with women and producing a giant offspring. (See: Genesis 6:4, Job 2:1, 2 Peter 2:4-6, Jude 6-7) The hand of God and man destroyed many, if not all, their seed. Jude 6-7 explains why no present-day attempts have been made to make giants (The fallen angels who did this were punished in everlasting chains under darkness. I believe this has served as a warning to every other angelic being.)

Deuteronomy 20:16-18 states: "But of the cities of these people which the Lord your God gives you as an inheritance, you shall let nothing that breathes remain alive, but you shall utterly destroy them: the Hittite and the Amorite and the Canaanite and the Perizzite and the Hivite and the

Jebusite, just as the Lord your God has commanded you, lest they teach you to do according to all their abominations which they have done for their gods, and you sin against the Lord your God."

Even so, we must destroy the giants and the many "ites" which are inhabiting our Promised Land. Make no peace with them. Show them no mercy. We must not leave room for them, but rather slay them. We must conquer whatever our giants may be. Slay fear and debt. Slay unbelief and lies. Destroy unforgiveness and bitterness. But how? Let us look at a few examples below of how God's Word says to take on these giants.

Begin with faith. Faith is the opposite of unbelief and will slay that giant. How does one get faith? "So then faith comes by hearing, and hearing by the word of God." (Romans 10:17) Hear God's Word and believe it. Read and listen to God's Word and meditate on it. Pray over it. Faith will be built in our hearts as we practice this discipline. Find and go to a church that preaches the Bible. As we listen to what God says, repent of any sins that He shows us and flee from doing those sins. God will help us overcome. Faith will then grow in our hearts. This scripture will come alive (Luke 1:37) "For with God nothing will be impossible" and in Mark 9:23 Jesus said to him, "If you can believe, all things are possible to him who believes."

What about fear? How does one kill the giant of fear? 1 John 4:18 says, "There is no fear in love; but perfect loves cast out fear..." Get love! How does one do that? 1 John 4:19 says, "We love Him because He first loved us." We must understand, meditate on, and receive God's love for us. John 3:16 says, "For God so loved the world, that he gave his only begotten Son, that whoever believes in him should not perish but have everlasting life." Love for God and man will always slay the giant of fear! The more we understand and receive God's love, the more we will love, and fear will cease in our life. Read 1 Corinthians 13 on God's definition of love and ask God for a fresh revelation of His love to fall on you.

What about the giant of unforgiveness? Unforgiveness is destroyed when a man receives God's forgiveness through Jesus Christ. It is easier to forgive others when we understand how much God has forgiven us when we did not deserve it. Forgiveness, much like love, is a choice. Choose to love, choose to forgive. By doing so, that giant falls, and freedom is ours.

There are many other giants. But know this, Jesus has the answers in how to slay them all! John 8:32 says, "And you shall know the truth, and the truth shall make you free." And John 17:17 states: "Sanctify them by Your truth; Your word is truth."

Jesus is the Good Shepherd. (John 10:11) Trust Him as your Shepherd, and let Him lead you to your Promised Land. He will give you instructions on how to slay the giants, to inherit your Promised Land. Look entirely to Jesus and trust Him to reveal to you what giants need to be taken down to inherit your Promise Land.

Father, give each of us Your vision for our Promised Land. Jesus leads us as the Good Shepherd into our Promised Land and helps us defeat all the giants that would try to keep us from our inheritance! We look to You. May Your Word grow faith in our heart to trust You to help us slay all of our giants. I ask this all of You Father, In Jesus' name, Amen.

JOURNAL/REFLECTIONS

1. What are the giants in your Promised Land?

___

2. How do you take down the giants in your land?

___

3. Why is it important to take ALL the giants down? (Deuteronomy 20:16-18)

Personal Prayer

12 SPIES

"Then they told him and said: 'We went to the land where you sent us. It truly flows with milk and honey, and this is its fruit. Nevertheless, the people who dwell in the land are strong; the cities are fortified and very large; moreover, we saw the descendants of Anak there.'" (Numbers 13:27-28, the descendants of Anak were the giants)

In Numbers, chapter 13, twelve men (one man for each tribe) are given the opportunity to spy out the Promised Land. What they see and how they communicate that to the others, will affect an entire nation. We, too, must have vision for our lives. How we see problems, obstacles, and roadblocks will affect those around us, for better or for worse. May God help us to see all hindrances to His promises through the eyes of faith, which says, "For with God nothing will be impossible." (Luke 1:37)

Ten of the twelve spies had no faith. They saw giants, obstacles, and roadblocks. They did not believe they could conquer the land and all that they had seen. They forgot about God, who delivered them from Egypt, parted the Red Sea, and fed them supernaturally in the desert. They did not believe God's promise. Instead, they doubted Him.

Numbers 13:30 says, "Then Caleb quieted the people before Moses, and said, 'Let us go up at once and take possession, for we are well able to overcome it.'" Caleb is a man of faith. He believes in God and knows God is bigger than the giants, the walled cities, and any obstacle. Caleb is ready for war. He knows God is with Him and is ready to enjoy the blessings of the land.

"But the men who had gone up with him said, 'We are not able to go up against the people, for they are stronger than we.'" (Numbers 14:31)

Any man can state the obvious. These men are faithless. They are not problem solvers, but the problem! It takes a special man to see with eyes of faith. With God's help, there is no giant too tall, no obstacle too strong, no challenge too big! But Jesus looked at them and said to them, "With men this is impossible, but with God all things are possible." (Matthew 19:26)

The ten faithless spies, their testimony to the people, was about the giants and how they were like grasshoppers! (Numbers 13:32-33) The people then lifted their voices and cried. They wept that night. Why? They believed in the faithless spies. Unbelief spread throughout the camp. Hopelessness infected the people. They were in such despair they wished they had died in Egypt or the wilderness and made plans to return to Egypt. Who in their right mind would want to go back to a place where they would be enslaved? That is what fear does! It keeps us from advancing. It robs us of God's promised blessings and keeps us, slaves.

Joshua and Caleb, the two good spies, respond by saying, "The land we passed through to spy out is exceedingly good land. If the Lord delights in us, then He will bring us into this land and give it to us, a land which flows with milk and honey. Only do not rebel against the Lord, nor fear the people of the land, for they are our bread; their protection has departed from the, and the Lord is with us. Do not fear them." (Numbers 14:7-9)

What faith in God they had, to even compare the giants to bread? Meaning: we will devour them, do not fear. Do you believe that? With God, our obstacle is bread; our giant is bread; our challenge is bread. With God, we will overcome. The people wanted to kill Joshua and Caleb.

(Numbers 14:10) Fear made them irrational, even murderous. They desired to murder the two men who told them the truth.

God would intervene and save the two faithful men, but He pronounced judgment on the nation. No one who was twenty years of age and older would be allowed to enter the Promised Land. They all would die in the wilderness, except for Joshua and Caleb. Only those two men out of hundreds of thousands, and possibly millions, were allowed to enter and possess their Promised Land.

Which ones are you? Do you believe God? Do you tell God how big your problems are, or do you tell your problems how big your God is? Are we men and women of faith or faithlessness? Do we inspire courage or fear? Is our sphere of influence better or worse because of us?

May God help us to trust Him, trust His Word, and Believe Him in the midst of every trial for His glory. No matter where you are at, whether full of faith, or little to no faith, let today be a brand-new day. Put your trust in Jesus and ask Him to grow your faith. Practice what the Scripture says in Hebrews 12:2, "looking unto Jesus, the author and finisher of our faith ..."

Father, thank You for Your Word! Thank You for Your power. Thank You that with God, nothing is impossible! Please help us be men like Joshua and Caleb! Help us to see Your Word and promises! Help us look at every giant, obstacle, and hindrance to our Promised Land through eyes of faith, so that we can conquer and inherit it and enjoy Your blessings! May our faith and actions affect those around us for good! Bless us for Your glory! I pray this in Jesus' name, Amen.

JOURNAL/REFLECTIONS

1. Numbers 13:30 says Caleb said they were more than able to overcome. How are you able to overcome the giants in your land?

_____
_____
_____
_____
_____
_____
_____
_____
_____
_____

2. According to Numbers 13:32-33, how did faithlessness, hopelessness, and unbelief affect the people and their situation?

_____
_____
_____
_____
_____
_____
_____
_____
_____
_____
_____

3. In contrast to faithlessness, hopelessness, and unbelief, how did the response of Caleb and Joshua in Numbers 14:7-9 differ? Which set of people are you? Do you tell God how big your problems are, or do you tell your problems how big your God is?

_____
_____
_____
_____
_____
_____
_____
_____
_____

Personal Prayer

_____
_____
_____
_____
_____
_____
_____
_____
_____
_____
_____
_____
_____

MARY MOMENTS

"But Martha was distracted with much serving. And she went up to him and said, 'Lord, do you not care that my sister has left me to serve alone? Tell her then to help me.'" But the Lord answered her, 'Martha, Martha, you are anxious and troubled about many things, but one thing is necessary. Mary has chosen the good portion, which will not be taken away from her.'" (Luke 10:40-42)

"Cinderelly, Cinderelly
Night and day, it's Cinderelly
Make the fire, fix the breakfast
Wash the dishes, do the mopping
And the sweeping and the dusting
They always keep her hopping
She goes around in circles till she's very, very dizzy. Still, they holler, "Keep a-busy, Cinderelly!"

Boy, I imagine these lyrics to Walt Disney's *Cinderella* sound a lot like what Martha might have been feeling that day in Luke chapter 10. Martha, at that moment, busy doing a plethora of things causing her to be troubled, worried, exhausted, and frustrated. Isn't that like us sometimes? So much to do and not enough time?

It is really easy to get caught up in the hustle and bustle of everything going on. I mean, let's be real; it is not that hard to do when we live in a culture that sets unrealistic expectations on how to live the perfect life. So, we set out to meet those unrealistic expectations by filling up our schedules with something every day of the week. We have five different parties to shop for and attend, three family gatherings to cook for, family photos, the monthly service project to participate in, and on top of life's regular demands. No time for rest. Just go, go, go, and do, do, do. The bottom line is, we are living in a "Martha World."

So, let us take a closer look at our key verses and see what we can learn from Martha and Mary. "But Martha was distracted with much serving. And she went up to him and said, 'Lord, do you not care that my sister has left me to serve alone? Tell her then to help me." (Luke 10:40) Like Martha, when we are overwhelmed and exhausted with the busyness of serving, it can cause our attitudes to take a detour south. The fruit produced from operating out of a state of anxiousness brings about frustration and steals our joy and peace in present moments. There is absolutely nothing wrong with working hard for Jesus, that is good.

The problem happens when we become distracted with much serving, because it causes us to be distracted from Jesus.

We can learn a valuable lesson from a moment Martha had here. You see, when Martha took her eyes off Jesus, she became irritated and frustrated in all her efforts to serve Jesus, and she began to criticize her sister, who she thought wasn't doing as "much" for the Lord as she was. We must not get so focus on our works for the Lord, but instead stay focused on who we are working for. But the Lord answered her, "Martha, Martha, you are anxious and troubled about many things, but one thing is necessary. Mary has chosen the good portion, which will not be taken away from her." (Luke 10:41-42) Mary made a priceless choice to step away from all the noise and get still before the Lord, and for that, she was commended. Like Mary, we must choose to find time daily to sit at the feet of Jesus and listen. That time of sitting at the feet of Jesus is an act of worship unto

Him, and it is in that time of worship that Jesus says we receive the good portion. (Luke 10:42)

That phrase "good portion" in the Greek is *chreia*. It means we receive such things as we need for sustenance and the journey. To supply what is necessary for life.

The time we spend with the Lord is extremely valuable to us. It is in time that He provides us with what is essential. It is just like our cars needing to be refueled to get us to the next place. Our spirits must be refueled also to journey on. In His Presence, at His feet, all the things we deal with in our "Martha World" like the fear, worry, stress, anxiety, sickness, and the feeling of heaviness has to go. Our "Mary Moments" allow Him to adjust our focus on what is necessary, good, and pleasing to Him. Like Mary, we need to be able to discern when to serve the Lord and when to sit with the Lord.

As this year unfolds and things ramp up, remember that Jesus longs to be gracious to you and show you compassion. (Isaiah 30:18) He rejoices over you with gladness and quiets you with His love. (Zephaniah 3:17) When we start to feel frustrated and overwhelmed, may we run to the feet of the One who can lift our head and give us what we need to continue forward?

Oh, that we will be children of the Lord who find "Mary Moments" in this "Martha World."

JOURNAL/REFLECTIONS

1. What has you distracted from spending time with Jesus? (Luke 10:40-42)

___

2. How has the culture influenced the "busyness" of your life?

___

A Closer Walk With Jesus

3. What is something you can learn from Mary and Martha?

_____
_____
_____
_____
_____
_____
_____
_____
_____

Personal Prayer

_____
_____
_____
_____
_____
_____
_____
_____
_____
_____
_____
_____
_____
_____
_____

THE GOOD SHEPHERD

"A Psalm of David. The LORD is my Shepherd; I shall not want." (Psalms 23:1)

A shepherd guides, protects, heals, nurtures, and knows His every sheep in His flock. Did you know the Bible tells us that Jesus is the Good Shepherd? If you are a child of God, then the Bible calls you one of His sheep. Jesus is the Good Shepherd (John 10:11); in fact, He laid down His life for His sheep. What love He has for us. His selfless act shows us we can trust Him because He is a faithful Shepherd. Let us take a closer look today at Psalm 23 and the characteristics of our Good Shepherd.

In our key verse, Psalms 23:1, the phrase, "I shall not want" speaks of the shepherd's provision for His flock so that His sheep have no lack or want of anything. He provides shelter, food, safety, and relationship. Everything that we the sheep need; our Shepherd gives us. Did you know we also are shepherds? As husbands or wives, fathers or mothers, in business, if you are a manager or have a leadership role, you too are a shepherd. May God help us to follow Christ's footsteps to shepherd those under our care faithfully! May we learn from Him how He does it.

Psalms 23:2 states that, "He makes me lie down in green pastures. He leads me beside still waters." As the Good Shepherd, Jesus leads His sheep to green pastures. He knows what is good for you and me. He makes us lie down, meaning Jesus Himself knows when to give rest to His sheep. Jesus knows the importance of rest and that we all need it. Our Good Shepherd leads us to green pastures on purpose. These green pastures are a picture of His provision for us and of our needs being taken care of. The still waters in verse 2 speak of our Shepherd's goodness. He does not lead us to the rapids or rushing water, which are dangerous, but by the still waters where we can take a drink, rest, and hear His voice. It is also in the still waters where a person can see their reflection. Take time to reflect on the goodness and faithfulness of Jesus in your life. May Jesus be our example as we lead those that He has given us to shepherd. May they experience green pastures of prosperity and safety and the goodness and refreshment of the still waters.

"He restores my soul. He leads me in paths of righteousness for His names sake." (Psalms 23:3) In this verse, He restores our soul. Our soul is our mind, our will, and our emotions. Did you know that our Shepherd restores our soul when we believe in Him at salvation? And He does not stop there, He continues to restore our mind, will, and emotions. That is part of lying down in the green pastures. Vision, ideas, and wisdom do not come when you are speeding down the freeway honking your horn at the guy who just cut you off! But they come when your mind is at rest, peaceful, in a time of reflection and communion with the Good Shepherd Jesus!

"Even though I walk through the valley of the shadow of death, I will fear no evil, for you are with me, your rod and your staff, they comfort me." (Psalms 23:4) According to this verse, we do not need to fear death if Jesus is our Shepherd. He already died for you and me, canceling out our sin, making a way for us to live forever with Him in eternity by believing in Him. Jesus never leaves nor forsakes His sheep. His rod can be used to discipline. Whoever is His, He disciplines. A good father always disciplines His children. The rod can also chase off Satan, evil, and danger from getting to you. His staff is to retrieve those who wander off and get lost. Because He is the Good Shepherd, if His sheep wander off into sin and darkness, Jesus will go after them in order to retrieve them and bring them back into the fold. (Luke 19:10) So, His rod and staff bring comfort.

"You prepare a table before me in the presence of my enemies; You anoint my head with oil; my cup overflows." (Psalms 23:5)

The enemies of His sheep will see the Shepherd's goodness, provision, and blessings poured out on the sheep. The anointing with oil and overflow speaks of God's goodness and blessings being so great that they overflow, which means those around the overflow also share in the abundance and blessings. May God cause our cups to overflow, so that those in our realm of influence get blessed with the overflow that He pours out on us.

"Surely goodness and mercy shall follow me all the days of my life, and I shall dwell in the house of the LORD forever." (Psalms 23:6)

Goodness and mercy follow His sheep. May all His sheep open their eyes and hearts to this precious truth, that no matter what or how we feel, God's goodness and mercy follow us all the days of our lives. As Jesus' sheep, our portion shall be to dwell in the house of the LORD forever. Amen!

Father, I thank You for Your Son, Jesus, the Good Shepherd! Help us all grow closer to Him in relationship. Help us all to look to Him for guidance, direction, and wisdom. May we all learn from Him and let Him shepherd us, and in doing so, learn to be shepherds to those who are under us! I ask all these things of You Father, in Jesus' name, Amen.

JOURNAL/REFLECTIONS

1. What verse from Psalm 23 speaks to you the most? Why?

___

2. How have you seen the Lord as "Shepherd" in your life?

___

3. Have you seen the goodness and mercy of God following you? If so, how?

_____
_____
_____
_____
_____
_____
_____
_____
_____
_____

Personal Prayer

_____
_____
_____
_____
_____
_____
_____
_____
_____
_____
_____
_____
_____
_____
_____

Bibliography

[i] Brown, Chris, Brock, Mack, Furtick, Steven, Redman, Matthew. *Do It Again*. Elevation Worship. Provident Label Group. 2017. www.providentlabelgroup.com.

[ii] Terkurst, Lisa. *Uninvited*. Nashville, Tennessee. Nelson Books. 2016.

[iii] Crowder, David. *Oh How He Loves Us*. Written by McMillan, John Mark. Integrity Hosanna Music. Capitol CMG Publishing. 2005. www.capitolcmgpublishing.com

[iv] "Mully". Sterling Light Productions. Bardis Productions. Director: Haze, Scott. 2015.

Bible versions used:

-Amplified Bible Classic Edition
-English Standard Version
-Message
-New American Standard 1977
-NIV
-NKJV
-KJV
-New Revised Standard

Definitions derived from the Oxford Dictionary

Devotionals & Websites used:

"Never the Same"
James W. Goll
elijahlist.com/mobile/display.word.html?ID=1840

"Follow the Instruction"
http://www.schultze.org/oldCTO280.HTML
https://www.beliefnet.com/faiths/christianity/10-epic-miracles-in-the-bible.aspx

"God Remembered"
gotquestions.org/God-remembered.html

"Jesus Was Rejected"
Courtney Writing
Chrisitanitytoday.com/women-leaders/2018/january/getting-past-the-lie-of-rejection.html

"Heavenly Exchange"
Helen Howarth Lemmel author of song: "Turn Your Eyes to Jesus"

"Sifted Like Wheat"
Career trend.com/jpw-does-4925686-farmers-sift-wheat.html

"Word vs. World"
https://www.christianity.com/bible/ww.php?d=2020-06-08
https://psychcentral.com/blog/love-is-a-choice-more-than-a-feeling/

"Do it Again"
https://westernusa.salvationarmy.org/usw_thq/news/the-christmas-story-a-babys-birth-that-saved-the-world/

"More Than You Can Handle"
https://churchleaders.com/outreach-missions/outreach-missions-articles/284416-god-will-give-can-handle-the-gospel-coalition-mitch-chase.html

About the Authors

Travis is an ordained minister and has traveled alongside an African evangelist where they ministered and preached in different churches throughout the United States and Zambia. He helped serve as part of the staff in a 24-7 house of prayer in North Idaho. He now works in the safety department for a utility company that builds power lines across the southern United States. He writes weekly devotionals for those interested within his company.

Tiffany has done mission's work in Mexico and Cambodia. She also served at the 24-7 prayer house in North Idaho and at the Dream Center in Salt Lake City, Utah. She has written for different blogs, as well as hosted Bible studies.

Travis and Tiffany were married in 2013, have three sons with another child on the way, and reside in Beaumont, Texas.